HERE'S YOUR ANSWER

HERE'S YOUR ANSWER

By

ROBERT J. LITTLE

❧ ❧ ❧
❧ ❧ ❧

MOODY MONTHLY

CHICAGO

Printed in the United States of America

CONTENTS

FOREWORD

To be curious, and even inquisitive, is natural. To want to know the how and why of things has characterized human beings of all ages. In order to be of service to its friends who desire biblical answers to their questions the Moody Bible Institute, through its radio voice, WMBI, has broadcast for many years what is known as "The Question Box." Happy is the man whose knowledge of the Word of God is such that he can give satisfactory and authoritative answers to the many questions which are submitted by listeners day after day. Such a man is Robert J. Little, affectionately known as "the radio pastor" of WMBI.

It is quite evident to all of us who know him that Mr. Little is gifted in a special way to give clear and simple answers to the questions submitted to him. Wherever possible to give "chapter and verse," he does so. Wherever there is room for honest difference of opinion, he states his own position, but always with due respect for those who may think otherwise. He is never dogmatic.

In order to preserve the results of his labor, and also to make them available to those who may not have opportunity to tune in, two hundred of these questions with their answers have been brought together under the general title, *Here's Your Answer* One has but to scan the index to see the wide range of subjects included, such as Birth Control, Cremation, Labor and Management, Outer Space, Tongues, and so on.

Included in the book are two helpful indexes, one to the biblical references and the other to topics referred to. These indexes will enable a reader to look up any subject or any Scripture verse dealt with in the book.

In this book busy pastors will find suggestions and source material for sermons that will meet the needs of many who, for one reason or another, might never put their questions into writing.

7

Students of sociology, likewise, may find here answers to some of their questions which are not dealt with in secular textbooks.

Here is a book which will not be read through and then laid aside, but one which will be consulted again and again as occasion requires. As one who has been greatly blessed by the ministry of its author, I take great pleasure in commending this book to all who have a desire to know the "how and why" of many things in this complex age, as revealed in the Book of books, the Holy Bible.

CARL ARMERDING, *President*
Central American Mission

BIBLE

1. What is the basis for the belief that the Bible is infallible?

The Bible claims to be a divine revelation, and thus would be infallible. Many times in the Old Testament we read the expression, "Thus saith the Lord." In Exodus 20:1 we read, "And God spake all these words." All the Bible writers claim that what they wrote was a message from God. The Apostle Paul wrote, "Now we have received, not the spirit of the world, but the Spirit which is of God; that we might know the things which are freely given to us of God. Which things also we speak, not in words which man's wisdom teacheth, but which the Holy Ghost teacheth; comparing spiritual things with spiritual" (I Cor. 2:12-13).

This text claims inspiration for the very words used. The Lord Jesus Himself went beyond inspiration of the words of Scripture when He said, "One jot or one tittle shall in no wise pass from the law, until all be fulfilled" (Matt. 5:18). The Apostle Peter testified, ". . . the prophecy came not in old time by the will of man; but holy men of God spake as they were moved by the Holy Ghost" (II Pet. 1:21). In II Timothy 3:16 the Apostle Paul wrote, "All scripture is given by inspiration of God . . ."

Much of what is contained in the Bible can be tested for accuracy, and probably no other book has been subjected to such close and repeated scrutiny as the Bible. Its historical statements have often been questioned, only to be confirmed by further research. Though written at a time when man's scientific knowledge was very limited, it does not contain any of the gross fallacies which were commonly held in those days. The Bible is not a treatise on scientific subjects, but it does not make statements contrary to any established facts of science. However, what the Bible says may be contrary to some theories held by certain scientists.

On the positive side, the fulfillment of many prophecies—often

9

given in considerable detail and contrary to the law of probabilities—indicates that they were given by divine revelation.

The very structure of the Bible is an evidence of its divine origin. Though the Bible was written over a period of approximately fifteen hundred years by a wide variety of authors, one can refer from one part to another and find a most wonderful unity. This indicates that behind the writers of the various parts of the Bible there was a single directing mind—the Holy Spirit.

There are many incidental proofs of the divine origin of the Bible which show its authority and reliability.

2. Since men wrote the Bible, how can Christians say it is the Word of God?

One of the mysteries of divine revelation is the question of how—and how far—the human element entered into the writing of Scripture. That God used the personality of the various writers is evident. An example of this is seen in the medical terminology used by Luke both in his Gospel and in the Acts of the Apostles. He was a physician, and used many terms commonly used by medical men in his day. The writings of Paul contain logical discourses not common to other writers. These men did not write as amanuenses—persons employed to write at the dictation of another.

On the other hand, we find in the Bible claims of divine guidance and revelation, and also disclaimers that the works produced were the products of the ingenuity of the writers. Moses, in giving the law, said, "And God spake all these words" (Exodus 20:1). Paul expressly claimed that the words he used to communicate the divine revelation given him were not of his own choice: "Which things also we speak, not in words which man's wisdom teacheth, but which the Holy Ghost teacheth" (I Cor. 2:13).

Perhaps the most precise definition is given in a modified translation of II Peter 1:21, a translation believed to be in accordance with the best attested text: "Men spoke from God, being borne along by the Holy Ghost." God used men to communicate His mind to mankind, not ignoring the instrument He was using, and yet He so guided that what was written was, in fact, the very Word of God. The result is that the Bible communicates its authority to the submissive and believing mind.

3. Can a modern reader take the Bible accounts of miracles literally?

Yes. The Bible has proved itself a reliable witness in its history and in the prophecies relating to time up to the present. We see no reason to doubt either its predictions concerning time yet future or its account of things in the past, including miracles.

Even in human experience men are able to do things today which would have been considered miraculous a few years ago. However, the miracles recorded in the Bible were not merely evidences of advanced knowledge but were demonstrations of divine power, and we accept them as such.

While God is not performing the same type of miracles today, there are miracles of His grace and in His providences which equal those recorded in the Bible in that they demand a power beyond the capacity of man. We believe that God still intervenes in human affairs as it pleases Him (Ps. 76:10).

4. Does not science discredit the Bible in some important respects?

I believe that when the Bible is rightly interpreted, no conflict will be found between science and the Bible, though men have sometimes misinterpreted the Bible in the light of the scientific knowledge available in their day. We do not know of any established *fact* of science which contradicts any truth in the Bible, though there are scientific *theories* which do so. The Bible has been a finished product for almost two thousand years. Science is constantly changing. If men had rewritten parts of the Bible to reconcile it with science a few years ago, it would have been an outdated book today.

The Bible is concerned primarily with God's dealings with man; science is concerned with the universe as it can be perceived by man's senses and understood by his mentality. The Bible does not purport to be a textbook on science; it treats of natural phenomena in an incidental way. The Bible reveals things which "eye hath not seen, nor ear heard, neither have entered into the heart of man" (I Cor. 2:9-16). These are things with which science cannot deal.

5. Why are there so many different interpretations of the Bible? Is not this confusing?

In view of the varied backgrounds from which we come, and our varying degrees of spiritual growth, it is remarkable that so great a degree of unity of thought is found among true believers in Christ. This is an evidence that they are indwelt by the same Holy Spirit who is the Author of the Book.

Concerning the basic truths of salvation, virtually all evangelical groups are in agreement. Obviously, a deeper knowledge of the Bible requires various forms of study, although it is amazing how persons with little learning can gain a deep insight into spiritual truth under the guidance of the Holy Spirit (I Cor. 2:12-15). If we approach the Bible in humility with a teachable spirit, using the helps available to us, we may be confident of growing in grace and in the knowledge of our Lord and Saviour Jesus Christ (II Pet. 3:18).

6. If the Bible is divinely inspired, why is it revised from time to time?

It is not the divinely inspired text which is revised, but translations from the copies which are available. None of the original writings are extant. In ancient times, all copying was done by hand, which has resulted in some variations in the copies. Sometimes marginal notes were made, and later copied into the text. Sometimes copyists inadvertently altered the text or omitted something. This is not surprising. It is rather amazing that the text is as fully authenticated as it is, so that for the most part, scholars and researchers are agreed as to it.

In the time when some of our earlier translations were made less material was available from which to make a translation than in later years when other manuscripts were discovered. Much research was done to obtain, as accurately as could be, the text of the original writing. Most of the discrepancies in the various copies are of minor importance, and we know of no major doctrine of Scripture which rests upon a disputed text.

Apart from the question of the text to be translated, there is another reason for revisions. Our usage of words changes with the passage of time. In any "living language" changes are constantly taking place, so that a word which properly translated the original a hundred years ago might not be a good translation today. An example is the use of the old English word *let*, which used to convey the meaning of hindering. Today it means the opposite. Revisions of translations enable us to have the Word of God expressed in the language we use today.

Another problem is one which is involved in all use of language: Words often have an ambiguous meaning, so that it is possible to take them in either of two or more meanings. One translator may have taken an expression in one sense, while another may see it in another light. We are often helped in understanding ambiguous expressions by considering the context in which the word is found. The passage may require a particular translation to convey the thought of the paragraph. Also, in cases where there is a question, we may sometimes find guidance from the use of the word elsewhere in Scripture, although this does not always follow, since it may be used elsewhere in a different context.

We find help in the guidance of the Holy Spirit, since He who inspired the writers of Scripture indwells every believer. In cases where the correct interpretation requires spiritual discernment, he is best fitted to make the translation who not only has the mental training in the languages but who is also indwelt by the Holy Spirit. To be divinely guided, the translator should be a deeply spiritual man.

The problem is not one of revision of the original writings but of the translations which convey the text of those writings in the languages used today.

7. Were there many writers of the Psalms?

There were several human writers of the Psalms, although in the New Testament the Holy Spirit is declared to be the divine Author in Acts 1:16 and in Hebrews 3:7. Acts 2:25, 30 shows that in Psalm 16 David wrote as a prophet, and II Peter 1:20 specifically asserts that the prophets were "moved" or "borne along" by the Holy Spirit in their writing. II Timothy 3:16 ascribes divine inspiration to "all Scripture," which includes the Psalms.

The *Wycliffe Commentary* states that the word *Psalms* is taken from the title to the compilation in the Septuagint translation, and adds that the Hebrews used a word in their language meaning "Praises." This commentary says: "In both the Hebrew and Greek terms there is the root meaning of playing instrumental music." In time the word took on the meaning of singing to musical accompaniment, a feature of Israelite worship made popular by the singing of the Levitical choirs. The Psalms are divided into five "books," and these were referred to by the Jews as the Pentateuch of David. It is thought by some that by divine guidance the Psalms were collected so that the several books would have some correspondence with the message of the five books of Moses.

As to authorship, this commentary notes that "All but 34 of the Psalms bear some type of title as a superscription . . . Among the titled psalms, 73 use the inscription *le Dawid*." This is usually translated "A Psalm of David," but can mean "belonging to David," or "concerning David," or something similar. Twelve are connected with Asaph, twelve with the sons of Korah, two with Solomon, one with Ethan, and one with Moses. Psalm 2 is one of the 34 which bear no title, but Acts 2:25 ascribes it to David.

BIBLICAL INTERPRETATION

8. If God created the earth in six days, where did the geologic ages come in?

In one view of the Scriptures the six days *were* the geologic ages. Others believe that the earth was created in a fully ordered state, and that it later became a chaos by the judgment of God, possibly at the time when Satan rebelled against God and introduced sin into the universe. Those holding this view believe the geologic ages occurred in connection with that chaotic state.

The late William Kelly suggested that Psalm 104:29-30 allows for the successive creation of differing forms of life which existed at a given time, and then became extinct. The passage says: "Thou hidest thy face, they are troubled: thou takest away their breath, they die, and return to their dust. Thou sendest forth thy Spirit, they are created; and thou renewest the face of the earth."

Whatever the circumstances may have been which were involved in the chaos of Genesis 1:2 (and volumes have been written about it), I take it that any successive ages of animal and plant life would have occurred during that period, and that the six days were the time when God formed the earth as a habitation for man. It is my belief that in the foreknowledge and foreplanning of God, He purposed that man was to be the distinctive creation made in His image and likeness. And, since God foresaw the incarnation of His Son, the eternal purpose of God was centered in Christ (Eph. 3:11).

9. **Does Genesis 1:2 indicate that the world was created as a chaotic mass, which was later formed into the ordered universe that we are familiar with?**

Various diverse views are held concerning the meaning of the Genesis account of creation. Some hold that verse 2 is a description of what was created in verse 1, and that the *days* mentioned in the balance of the chapter are "ages." This view involves what is called "theistic evolution," which means an evolutionary process designed by God and operated by His power. This view does not involve the evolution of man from a lower order of being, since those who hold theistic evolution consider man's creation to be a direct act of God. Many Christian scholars hold this view.

Others view verse 1 of Genesis 1 as describing a complete creation, in an ordered form, which later became the chaos described in verse 2. The word translated "was" in verse 2 can mean "became." The words translated "without form and void" are alliterative in Hebrew: *tohu* and *bohu*. The first of these is found in Isaiah 45:18, where we read, "For thus saith the LORD that created the heavens; God himself that formed the earth and made it; he hath established it, he created it not in vain, he formed it to be inhabited." The word translated "in vain" is the same as that translated "without form" in Genesis 1:2. This is taken by some as a positive statement that Genesis 1:2 does not describe the original creation of the universe.

10. **What is meant by such terms as "the stone age," "the bronze age," and so on, and where do we read of these in the Bible?**

These terms have nothing to do with the geologic ages, but relate to periods supposed to mark the development of human civilization. It is thought that primitive man first learned to make tools of what was available to him, such as wood and stone. A stone would be fastened to the end of a stick by thongs, and then used as an axe or hammer. Later, it is thought, men discovered how to smelt ore, and developed the use of iron and copper, later making alloys of various metals.

Others believe that Adam was created with vast intelligence, and that even when driven from the garden of Eden he already possessed a high degree of knowledge, and was far from being a savage. Those holding this view believe that there was, before the flood, a highly developed civilization which was destroyed in the flood. Since the human family was then reduced to a small number, and these were soon scattered over the earth, much knowledge was lost, although archaeology shows that men from a very early date had highly developed skills.

We do not know of any way to account for the fact that some races and nations retained a civilized order while others lapsed into savagery, but the development of the human race after the Tower of Babel was not uniform. The Bible does not treat of this side of things, but we know there are places on the earth today where people live in a very primitive way, almost comparable to the "stone age." It is questionable whether the human race as a whole was ever, after the Tower of Babel, uniform in the degree of civilization achieved. Such expressions as "stone age" would not, in that case, have universal application, but would refer to the particular areas and periods where they had relevancy.

11. Who are "the sons of God" and the "daughters of men" referred to in Genesis 6:4-5?

These verses say: "There were giants in the earth in those days; and also after that, when the sons of God came in unto the daughters of men, and they bare children to them, the same became mighty men which were of old, men of renown. And GOD saw that the wickedness of man was great in the earth, and that every imagination of the thoughts of his heart was only evil continually."

Scholars differ in their views of the meaning of this text. It appears that the condition described resulted in the flood, and so was something far more serious than the sins common to man. But many consider that the "sons of God" were the descendants of Seth, who were believers, and that the "daughters of men" were the descendants of Cain, who were unconverted. It is considered that the mingling of believers with unbelievers would have led to the obliteration of a knowledge of the true God in the earth, because the ungodly women of Cain's line corrupted the godly men of Seth's line, resulting in an immoral mode of life.

To me this seems superficial, although many scholars take that view. It seems strange that it was the men who were godly, and the women ungodly; that all of the house of Seth were believers and that none of the women of Cain's line were believers. It seems strange, too, that these men all chose ungodly wives, or at least in sufficient number and proportion to bring about the judgment of the flood. Also, the intermarriage of believers with unbelievers would not produce a race of giants, or necessarily "men of renown."

The other view adopted also has difficulties, so it is not a case of one view being perfectly clear, and the other manifestly false. If that were so, there would be no difference of view.

It seems to me that the difficulties of the second view are more resolvable than those of the other. In this second view the "sons of God" represent fallen angels who took upon them a human form. Of course it is at once argued that this is impossible, but we know that in some cases angels did take human form. We cannot know the circumstances, nor the limitations, but wherever angels appeared in human form it was always as men, and never as women. This would account for the "sons of God" being all of one classification sexually, and would also indicate the contrast with "the daughters of men."

In the Old Testament believers were not called "sons of God" except in one passage, and that is prophetical. However, angels are referred to as "sons of God" in the Book of Job. In this case, the "daughters of men" would not mean only descendants of Cain, but any woman of Adam's race, of whatever particular family. If the bodies of these "men" were exceptional, as seems probable, they would have been attractive to most women; and their offspring may well have been "giants," "men of renown."

This would have been a corruption of the human race, and stories about these "men of renown" may have been the source from which came the mythological stories which abounded in later times. This corruption of humanity is thought by many to be referred to in II Peter 2:4 and Jude 6, where we read of a special group of fallen angels who "left their proper habitation," and are now kept in chains under darkness. This is not true of the "demons," who regularly roam the earth, according to the New Testament. There seem to be two distinct classes of fallen angels, one of which is free, the other bound. Such a mingling of different orders of creation might well have brought on the universal flood, and it may be significant that Noah was described in Genesis 6 as "perfect in his generations."

However, I do not think we should be dogmatic about it. Many Bible scholars prefer the first view.

12. Who was the first Gentile?

It would be easier to identify the first Jew, although that word needs definition also. Up until the call of Abram, God treated humanity as one, but when God gave to Abram the promise recorded in Genesis 12:1-3, he (and by implication, his posterity) was marked out as one set apart to God. The rest of the nations or peoples became, by that act, the goyim, or Gentiles ("nations"). Later scriptures explicitly included Abraham's posterity but limited the promise to the seed of Isaac (Gen. 17:19). Later still, this promise was confirmed to the posterity of Jacob (Gen. 28:14) and to Judah (Gen. 49:10).

In later history the descendants of the twelve sons of Jacob developed into twelve tribes, and eventually these became two kingdoms—the ten-tribe kingdom of Israel and the two-tribe kingdom of Judah. The name Judah was corrupted to "Jew," and at first was applied only to members of the two-tribe kingdom. But in later years it was applied to all of Israel indiscriminately. An example of this is found in Romans 2:28-29, where the Apostle Paul wrote, "For he is not a Jew, which is one outwardly; neither is that circumcision, which is outward in the flesh: but he is a Jew, which is one inwardly; and circumcision is that of the heart, in the spirit, and not in the letter; whose praise is not of men, but of God."

In a strict sense we cannot say Abraham was a "Jew," because that term did not come into vogue until long after his time. He was a Hebrew, though it is believed that this designation did not originate with him. After his time it seems to have been applied only to his posterity.

So, it was the call of Abram that resulted in the rest of the world becoming known as *goyim*, or Gentiles. There was no *first* Gentile.

13. Who are the ten lost tribes of Israel, and do they have existence at this time?

The expression "ten lost tribes of Israel" refers to the fact that more than 700 years before Christ the northern ten-tribe kingdom of Israel (after the division of the nation in the days of Rehoboam) was taken captive into Assyria, and never made a formal return to their land, as did the two-tribe kingdom of Judah (from Babylon about the year 536 B.C.). Some have surmised that the ten tribes still exist, more or less retaining their identity, and that at a future time they will be revealed.

Others believe that many individuals of these tribes did, in the course of time, return to Palestine, and became amalgamated with those who were in the land at that time. So while there was not a formal return, yet representatives of all twelve tribes were in the land at the time of the Lord. The rest of the members of the ten tribes are believed to have been scattered throughout the earth after the dissolution of the Assyrian empire. If this be true, there is not any group which can be identified as the "ten lost tribes of Israel."

This view seems confirmed by the language of both Paul and James. The former, making his defense before Agrippa, referred to "the hope of the promise made of God unto our fathers: unto which promise our twelve tribes, instantly serving God day and night, hope to come" (Acts 26:6-7). James addressed his epistle to "the twelve tribes which are scattered abroad." From this it would appear that neither Paul nor James knew anything about any "ten lost tribes."

14. Is there any biblical basis for considering that Great Britain is the "Israel" of the Bible, and that Britain and the United States together occupy the places respectively of Ephraim and Manasseh?

This question refers to a theory, held by some, which is known as British- or Anglo-Israelism. I do not know of any biblical basis for it. According to the claims of some, one of the sons of Saul, the first king of Israel, found his way to Great Britain, and married a princess of the people living there. This is supposed to link the entire British and American peoples with the promises of God made to Israel. Others have other theories, making the throne of David to be the throne of Britain. Somewhat similar theories, diverse in detail, are held by various groups.

The Bible presents a continuous history of the nation of Israel in Palestine, apart from the people being taken into captivity, and later scattered among the nations. When Judah returned from its Babylonian captivity, members of all the tribes were present, and we read of Ezra making "a sin-offering for all Israel, twelve he goats, according to the number of the tribes of Israel" (Ezra 6: 17). Several New Testament scriptures refer to the twelve tribes. (See Acts 26:7; James 1:1.) The Lord Jesus spoke of "the lost sheep of the house of Israel" (Matt. 10:6). This was at a time when, according to the theory under discussion, Britain was to be considered Israel, but Christ obviously referred to those in Palestine, or whose national interest centered there. A full discussion is found in various books on cults, but we believe there is no true biblical basis for the belief.

15. What is meant by the reference, in I Timothy 2:14-15, to the woman being saved in childbearing?

These verses read: "And Adam was not deceived, but the woman being deceived was in the transgression. Notwithstanding she shall be saved in childbearing, if they continue in faith and charity [love] and holiness with sobriety."

Four different meanings are commonly given to this passage.

The first two I consider definitely wrong. The latter two seem to me to be tenable, though I think the last is probably the intended meaning of the text.

The first, and perhaps most commonly taken meaning, is that if a woman dies giving birth to a child, she is assured of heaven. This is a serious misconception, for bearing children, or giving one's life in the process, is not the way of salvation. No one is saved apart from Christ's atonement and faith in Him. "Except a man be born again, he cannot see the kingdom of God," Jesus said.

A second sense often taken from the text is this: If a Christian woman (and perhaps her husband also) are believers in Christ and obedient to His will, the wife will be spared serious pain in childbearing, and is assured she will not die in this experience. This view is not in accord with the facts. Many ungodly women give birth to children with a minimum of discomfort, while many godly women suffer severely, and some have died in childbirth.

A third meaning has some measure of support in the context. It is this: Since the woman was the means of bringing sin into the world (v. 14), God ordained that through a woman the Saviour should be brought into the world. Some translate verse 15 in this way: "She shall be saved through her childbearing." This is true, whether it is the meaning of this passage or not. If we take it to be the meaning, then the restrictive clause, "if they continue in faith and love and holiness with sobriety," would indicate that personal faith is required for the individual to participate in that salvation.

The fourth view seems to me to be the intended one. The word *saved* can be translated "preserved." When Adam and Eve first fell into sin, God pronounced a specific judgment on each of them. We learn from experience that these judgments were not purely punitive but were also preservative. Sinful man cannot be trusted with leisure to the same degree as when there was no sin. Both men and women need to be occupied. God so ordered things that the man would be occupied working for a living; and the woman by bringing up a family, with multiplied conceptions, and hence a large family to care for (Gen. 3).

This view finds support in chapter 5 of this epistle, where Paul shows that a woman without adequate responsibility can easily be beguiled by Satan. Of course, men can be too. God did not intend that there should be a battle of the sexes, but all of us are to be on guard against Satan. We believe that the acceptance of this judgment from God does much to keep our lives on an ordered, godly basis, provided, of course, that we are believers in Christ.

16. Did the Africans inherit the curse on Ham?

The question implies some common misconceptions. While it appears that the black race sprang from Ham, not all the descendants of Ham were black. He had several sons. The name Ham means "dark" or "swarthy," and Cush, the name of his oldest son, means "black," but the Cushites, according to Genesis 10:7-12, settled the land of Shinar and became the beginning of the later Assyrian and Babylonian empires.

Also, although Ham was involved in the sin against his father, according to Genesis 9:22, the curse which Noah pronounced was not on Ham, but on Canaan, his youngest son. The entire incident is purposely stated in an obscure manner, but there is no suggestion of the curse being pronounced on Ham. Neither is there any suggestion that there is any relationship between this curse and the color of any of the races, whether red, black, brown, yellow, or white.

Neither does history support the idea that slavery originated with white people conquering black people. In the early days of human history it was not uncommon for a victor in military conflict to enslave conquered peoples, whatever the color of either nation. Professional men, such as doctors and men of letters, might be found in slavery. Also, black people sometimes enslaved other black people. Slavery does not represent a conflict between color races among men. It is rather the outworking of sin in man's nature which leads him to oppress others, instead of loving them and seeking their good.

If the curse upon Canaan was inherited by his offspring, as

seems implied in the text, this does not relate to the Africans. The descendants of this Canaan are identified in Genesis 10:15-19 as the inhabitants of what was later called "the land of Canaan." These are the tribes which became so corrupt that Joshua was commanded to destroy all of them when he entered that land. Of these cities it was said, "Thou shalt save alive nothing that breatheth" (Deut. 20:16-18). Insofar as this command was carried out, this would have ended the specific curse pronounced by Noah in Genesis 9.

17. What is the origin of the sabbath, and why was it observed only by the nation of Israel?

The first mention of the sabbath by that name is in Exodus 16:23, although we read in Genesis 2:2-3 that because God finished the ordering of the earth for man in six days, He rested on the seventh, and hallowed that day. There is no instruction to observe it, and I do not know of any reference in the Bible which indicates that it was observed, until the incident recorded in Exodus 16. There in connection with the giving of the manna, Moses instructed Israel to observe the day (v. 23). He said, in verse 29, ". . . the LORD hath given you the sabbath." This seems to indicate that the sabbath had not been observed prior to that.

In Exodus 20 this observance was incorporated in the Ten Commandments. Later, Nehemiah, in recounting God's goodness in calling Israel to be His people, said, in a prayer of confession to the Lord, "Thou camest down on Mount Sinai, . . . and madest known unto them thy holy sabbath, and commandedst them precepts, statutes and laws by the hand of Moses" (9:13-14).

While Moses was on Mount Sinai God said to Moses, "Speak thou also unto the children of Israel, saying, Verily, my sabbaths ye shall keep: for it is a sign between me and you throughout your generations; that ye may know that I am the LORD that doth sanctify you. . . . Wherefore the children of Israel shall keep the sabbath, to observe the sabbath throughout their generations, for a perpetual covenant. It is a sign between me and the children of Israel for ever" (Exodus 31:13, 16-17). These words are self-explanatory, and show that the keeping of the sabbath was one of several marks given the children of Israel to show they were the covenant people of God.

18. How and when was the sabbath changed to Sunday?

It is not strictly true that the sabbath was changed. It was given to Israel as the distinctive mark of their covenant relationship with God under law. Present-day Christians are not under the law of Moses as a basis of covenant relationship with God, though they are under the law of Christ (I Cor. 9:21; Gal. 6:2). While the New Testament contains several references to the sabbath, these refer to Israel's observance of the day and to the fact that some who became believers continued the practice. This is the subject of Romans 14, where Christians who held differing views about sabbath observance were told that the observance of special days was not fundamental to the Christian faith. There is no instruction in the New Testament to observe the sabbath day.

However, many believe that apart from the fact that the sabbath was the mark of Israel's covenant relationship with God, it was also a provision of God to make a break in man's work schedule, so that he could devote one day each week to the Lord's interests in a special way. We believe this is true. And it seems significant that in the New Testament the first day of the week is mentioned several times in connection with spiritual activities. Some have therefore called the first day of the week "the Christian Sabbath," but we believe this term is misleading, since Scripture does not use that expression, and it blurs the distinction between Israel and the church. We believe a better term is "the Lord's day," an expression found in Revelation 1:10. And while it is not specified that this was the first day of the week, many believe this is implied.

Even in the Old Testament "the morrow after the sabbath" had a special place in some connections, and since Christ rose on the first day of the week, it seems the appropriate day to devote to the Lord in this dispensation. It seems symbolic that

Christians begin the week with God on the basis of the atonement of Christ, whereas under the law the sabbath symbolized rest after labor, and so was more appropriate to the age of law and works. We do well to note that "by deeds of the law there shall no flesh be justified in his sight"(Rom. 3:20). But what the law could not do, Christ accomplished by His atonement (Acts 13:38-39).

That Christians are not under the law as a covenant was made clear by Christ when He instituted the Lord's Supper, and said, "This cup is the new testament [covenant] in my blood, which is shed for you" (Luke 22:20). Hebrews 8:13 shows that when the Lord spoke of a new covenant, He signified the end of the old. So we are not under that covenant of which the sabbath was the symbol.

19. If the church is not a continuation of Israel, is there any continuity in the work of God in men in the different dispensations?

Yes, there are several aspects of the work of God in men which are not dependent on the dispensation in which they live. From the beginning there has been the work of new birth, which introduces the believer into the family of God. This does not change with any alteration of God's governmental dealings with men. We must recognize that in Israel there were two aspects of things: one was outward, and the other inward. Every Israelite was a member of God's chosen race by natural birth; but none were members of God's spiritual family unless they were born again, as many scriptures show. (See Rom. 2:28-29; 9:6-8.)

In the family of God, one's circumstances vary greatly according to the time in which one lives. There were those who lived before the nation of Israel was formed who were God's children, but God dealt with them differently than with His people in the nation of Israel. Likewise, now that the nation is set aside, God is dealing with men in a different way, although the basic need of the new birth is the same for vital relationship to Him. Many prophecies indicate that in a future day God will again take up the nation of Israel, and deal with men differently than He does in the present order of things. The work of God in salvation is continuous; His governmental ways vary.

20. What is the meaning of "tithing," and what is its origin?

The word *tithe* means "a tenth," and is used in Scripture for the custom of giving a tenth of one's income or increase to the Lord. The first mention of tithing was on the occasion of Abraham's return from the slaughter of the kings (Genesis 14), when he met Melchizedek, king of Salem, priest of the Most High God. Abraham evidently felt that he owed his victory to God, and so he voluntarily rendered to Melchizedek tithes of all the spoil taken in battle.

Later, in the law given to Israel, God, through Moses, commanded every Israelite to render to Jehovah a tenth of all his increase, which then was chiefly in cattle and produce of the field. This was confirmed in Numbers 18, Deuteronomy 12, and other passages. In Malachi 3:8-10 Israel was accused of robbing God because they failed to give the full tithe required.

In the New Testament there is no specific *law* of tithing, but this does not imply that we Christians are to give less than was required of the Israelites. Rather, it is implied that we should give more, because the grace of God to us is more fully revealed. While the tithe is not mentioned as such (except as having reference to Israel), proportionate giving is clearly taught in I Corinthians 16:2: "Upon the first day of the week let every one of you lay by him in store as God hath prospered him." Much is said about giving liberally and joyfully, and II Corinthians 9:6-8 teaches that rewards in the day of Christ will be commensurate with the degree of our sacrificial giving now.

21. Is a person who has a very limited income expected to tithe?

Actually, the value of what we give to God lies in the measure of sacrifice involved. In the case of the widow's mites, we see a person whose gift was the smallest possible (except that she could have given one instead of two mites). However, the coins were the smallest in use at that time. Yet the Lord Jesus said of her, "This poor widow hath cast more in, than all they that have cast into the treasury" (Mark 12:43). I take this to mean that her gift counted for more in the sight of God than the gifts of all the others combined.

Another way of looking at the meaning of our Lord's words would be that all that had been put into the treasury was not worth two mites, because it had not involved that much sacrifice. The widow cast in her living for that day—a real sacrifice for her! Throughout Scripture the emphasis is on sacrificial giving, whether of time, talent, energy, or money. No matter what we offer to God, the value of our giving lies in how much it takes out of us.

II Corinthians 8:9 gives us the example of the Lord Jesus, who, "though he was rich, yet for your sakes he became poor, that ye through his poverty might be rich." Following the pattern of this perfect example, we read of the church of Macedonia that "in a great trial of affliction the abundance of their joy and their deep poverty abounded unto the riches of their liberality" (II Cor. 8:2). To fail to give because we do not have much is to rob ourselves of the joy and blessing of giving. However, II Corinthians 9:7 shows that our gifts must be made willingly if they are to find acceptance with God. One Christian cannot tell another what he should give.

22. **Ananias, speaking to Saul (Paul), following the confrontation by the Lord on the way to Damascus, said, "Rise and be baptized, and wash away thy sins" (Acts 22:16). How are we to take this?**

A. T. Robertson, in his *Word Pictures of the New Testament*, says: "Submit yourself to baptism. So as to *apolousai*, get washed off as in I Cor. 6:11. It is possible, as in Acts 2:38, to take these words as teaching baptismal remission or salvation by means of baptism, but to do so is in my opinion a complete subversion of

Paul's vivid and picturesque language. As in Rom. 6:4-6 where baptism is the picture of death, burial and resurrection, so here baptism pictures the change that had already taken place when Paul surrendered to Jesus on the way (Acts 22:10). Baptism here pictures the washing away of sins by the blood of Christ."

It is noteworthy that Acts 22:16 adds, "calling on the name of the Lord," for it is this which is said in Romans 10:13 to secure our salvation, of which baptism is at once the confession and the symbol. Bearing in mind that II Peter 1:20 states that no scripture is of its own solution (Newberry Bible margin), it is inevitable, as A. T. Robertson states, that we shall understand this verse in the light of what we are taught throughout the New Testament. It is the view of many that baptism, both here and in Acts 2:38, was simply the means whereby Christ's name was publicly confessed.

The Jamieson, Fausset and Brown Commentary, speaking about the words "be baptized and wash away thy sins," says, "Remission of sins is obtained solely through faith in the Lord Jesus, . . . but baptism being the visible seal of this, it is here and elsewhere naturally transferred from the inward act of faith to that which publicly and formally proclaimed it." The words "calling on the name of the Lord" receive this comment: " 'having (that is, after having) called on,' referring to the confession of Christ which *preceded* baptism." An example of such confession is found in Acts 8:37, though many critical versions omit this verse.

The Charles B. Williams version of Acts 22:16 reads, "Get up and be baptized and wash away your sins by calling on His name," with a footnote that the word *calling* is an adverbial participle of means. Ronald Knox has, "at the invocation of his name." The Berkeley version inverts the clauses and reads: "Rise; be baptized, and, calling on His name, be cleansed of your sins." Here, as elsewhere in the New Testament, it seems clear that while baptism was the visible confession before men, it was the inward calling upon Christ's name by faith which procured the remission of sins, as stated in Romans 10:9-13.

23. Why was Jesus baptized, since John's baptism implied repentance for sin?

John the Baptist himself questioned the propriety of his baptizing Jesus, but Scripture gives two reasons for His submitting to this rite. His answer to John was, "Suffer it to be so now, for thus it becometh us to fulfil all righteousness" (Matt. 3:15). John in his ministry had been calling on the nation to repent of its sins, and the people who were baptized did so as an outward expression of their repentance. The Lord Jesus had no sins of which to repent, but we believe He accepted baptism at John's hand to associate Himself publicly with those who were taking this step. His baptism was, in a sense, an identification of Himself with them as a pledge that He would take their place in the judgment. It was something like His putting His hand on the leper when He cleansed him. Christ died as our substitute on the cross.

But there was another important reason for His being baptized. In John 1 we are told that John the Baptist did not know who was the Son of God, so that while he evidently knew something about Jesus, he had to learn that He was the Son of God. He was told that the Holy Spirit would descend and abide upon the One who was the Son of God. This happened when Jesus was baptized, and because of this sign John was able to declare to the nation, "I saw, and bare record that this is the Son of God" (John 1:34).

24. Does the use of the word "likewise" in Luke 13:1-5 imply that these Galileans perished because of lack of repentance?

We believe that the Lord Jesus used the word *likewise* with reference to the fact of perishing, though it appears that the "perishing" in the case of those to whom he was speaking was in the deeper sense of being lost in their sins. The incident was an interesting one. Evidently, some time previous to this some Galileans had displeased Pilate, and had possibly been guilty of insurrection. Pilate retaliated by killing some of them as they were engaged in the very act of offering sacrifice to God. Thus their blood was mingled with that of their sacrifices.

Those who told Jesus about this incident were evidently Judeans, who held Galileans somewhat in contempt, and no doubt related the event to the Lord with the intimation that this was the judgment of God upon them. The Judeans may also have implied some measure of contempt for Jesus, since He had come from Galilee (although He had been born in Bethlehem and was of the tribe of Judah). The Lord's answer made it clear that such incidents did not indicate that those who suffered death were sinners above others. In fact, it is true today that when a disaster strikes it affects the godly as well as the ungodly.

But the Lord used the occasion to remind His audience of the greater disaster which lies ahead for all who do not repent of their sins, which implies coming to Him for salvation. Further, He mentioned an incident which had happened in Judea—and quite recently, we take it, since it appears to have been fresh in their memory. The incident took place in the very city of Jerusalem, and again the Lord made the point that those who suffered disaster were not more under the condemnation of God than others. Also He repeated His warning: "Except ye repent, ye shall all likewise perish," obviously referring to their being eternally lost. Some have connected His remarks with the destruction of Jerusalem, which occurred about A.D. 70. If this is involved, it seems to me this judgment is secondary to the fact of the eternal judgment of God.

25. **Why should the Lord say, in Luke 11:50-51, "That the blood of all the prophets, which was shed from the foundation of the world, may be required of this generation; from the blood of Abel unto the blood of Zacharias, which perished between the altar and the temple: verily I say unto you, It shall be required of this generation"?**

A similar statement appears in Matthew 23:35-36, with some slight variations, including these words: "all the righteous blood shed upon the earth." There are difficulties in the verse, such as identifying the particular Zacharias referred to, but I take it that our querist is asking why "this generation" should be held accountable for "all the righteous blood shed upon the earth" up to that time?

First, let me say what I think it does *not* mean. The Lord is not saying that in eternity the people of that generation would bear the guilt of all who had shed righteous blood before them. Scripture is very emphatic in teaching that "every one of us shall give account of himself to God" (Rom. 14:12), though the guilt of those of that particular generation might be augmented because of their perpetuating the commission of wrongs.

I take it that the Lord was going to deal with that generation in the sense of a national visitation, and this seems indicated by the verses which follow, Matthew 23:37-38. When the judgment of God fell on that nation, they lost their temple and ritual as well as their status as a nation. What has happened to them was described by the prophet Hosea (3:4): "For the children of Israel shall abide many days without a king, and without a prince, and without a sacrifice, and without an image, and without an ephod, and without teraphim."

The last is as significant as the first, because, though they would not have their religious center, yet it is stated that they would not turn to idolatry during that period. And they have not done so. Hosea 3:5 gives the promise of restoration: "Afterward shall the children of Israel return, and seek the LORD their God, and David their king; and shall fear the LORD and his goodness in the latter days." We believe this looks forward to the Messianic kingdom promised in many scriptures.

26. Is conscience a safe guide?

Violation of conscience makes us wrong, but the fact that we have a good conscience does not guarantee that we are right. Romans 14:14 says, "To him that esteemeth anything to be unclean, to him it is unclean," and verse 23 says, "Whatsoever is not of faith is sin." But conscience needs to be instructed, and it can be corrupted, so it is not always a safe guide.

Our English word *conscience* comes to us from the Latin, but has the same meaning as the Greek word which it translates: "to know within one's self." It signifies an awareness of the rightness or wrongness of what we do or desire. We do not find the word *conscience* in the Old Testament, though the idea is found there. After the sin of Adam and Eve, "the LORD God said, Behold the man is become as one of us, to know good and evil" (Gen. 3:22). Before they sinned, they were in a state of innocence, knowing the commandment of God, but having no knowledge of evil.

From Adam to Moses men "had not sinned after the similitude of Adam's transgression" (Rom. 5:14). That is, they had no divine commandment. Yet they knew right from wrong. For instance, when Joseph was tempted by Potiphar's wife to commit sin, he firmly replied, "How can I do this great wickedness, and sin against God?" He did not need a divine revelation to know that adultery was a sin against God; his own conscience told him that.

I Timothy 1:5 tells us that "a good conscience" is one of the requirements for Christian living, and at the end of that chapter we read of two men who, having put away a good conscience concerning the faith, "made shipwreck." A "weak conscience" may cause a person to feel condemned, because of tradition, about something which is not wrong in itself. Further instruction may correct this, but to violate his conscience meantime would be sin.

In Titus 1:15 Paul says of some that "even their mind and conscience is defiled," and in I Timothy 4:2 he speaks of others as "having their conscience seared with a hot iron." A "defiled conscience" condemns us when we practice things we know (or believe) are wrong. This is not a "guilt complex," as some call it; it is *guilt*—sin. A seared conscience is one habitually violated, so that it no longer warns of evil but can actually approve what God condemns.

In contrast with this is "a pure conscience," with which Paul said (in I Tim. 1:3) he served God. Even when he opposed Christianity, he believed what he was doing was right. This is an illustration of why conscience is not a safe guide unless it is enlightened by a right understanding of God's will. Earlier, in Acts 23:1, Paul had stated: "I have lived in all good conscience before God unto this day." In Acts 24:16 we read that Paul, in his speech of defense before Felix, said that it was his standing rule of life to exercise himself "to have always a conscience void of offence toward God, and toward men." And this rule is a good one for us.

27. Does God sanction segregation of the races?

Very little is said in the Bible about the division of humanity into color races. A text frequently mentioned in this connection is Acts 17:26: "And hath made of one blood all nations of men for to dwell on all the face of the earth, and hath determined the times before appointed, and the bounds of their habitation." The verse preceding this one states that it is God who gives to all "life, and breath, and all things." The wording of verse 26 in the Greek is not certain. The *New Bible Commentary* states, "The best texts omit 'blood'; the reference will then be to the 'one man' from whom, in the Bible, all men are descended. This contradicted the cherished Athenian belief that they themselves were sprung from the soil of Attica."

But whether we read the text "of one blood," or "of one" (meaning "of one man," or "one couple"), the resulting sense is that all humanity sprang from a common source. There is, therefore, no basic distinction in the races of mankind before God. All sprang from Adam and Eve, and all share the sinful nature which Adam communicated to his posterity. This question may be answered biologically, theologically, and sociologically.

Biologically, people of various color races have intermarried in every conceivable combination, and the resulting offspring show that there is no biological obstacle.

Theologically, Christ died for all, and John 3:16 tells us that "whosoever believeth on him shall not perish, but have everlasting life." The gospel message is for all men, and everyone who believes becomes a child of God by faith in Jesus Christ. Further, in this dispensation, all believers are made "one body" in Christ. Galatians 3:28 says, "There is neither Jew nor Greek, there is neither bond nor free, there is neither male nor female: for ye are all one in Christ Jesus."

Sociologically, there are problems arising out of strong antipathies, not only between color races but also between members of different nations of the same color race. With regard to *national* divisions, verse 26 of Acts 17 goes on to tell us that God "hath determined the times before appointed, and the bounds of their habitation." The "times" suggests the rise and fall of nations, as we read in Job 12:23, "He increaseth the nations, and destroyeth them: he enlargeth the nations, and straiteneth them again."

"The bounds of their habitation" seems to apply, in this text, to the various nations. See also Deuteronomy 32:8: "When the Most High divided to the nations their inheritance, when he separated the sons of Adam, he set the bounds of the people according to the number of the children of Israel." These texts indicate that God maintains an overall control of the nations, their territories, and their rise and fall. This is a truth which we should remember in connection with national affairs.

While these verses refer to "nations" rather than color races, it is a fact of history and geography that, in the providence of God, the yellow race occupied China and Japan; the brown race, lower Asia and Polynesia; the black race, Africa; and the white race, Europe; while what we call the red race occupied the Americas. Through man's devices—sometimes benevolent, sometimes malicious—the races have become intermingled, and it is now no more possible to segregate them than it would be to unscramble an egg, and get it back into its shell.

The Bible gives no specific instruction in the matter of race relations any more than it does about slavery; but it inculcates principles of conduct and individual character which, when practiced, not only eliminate slavery but enable people of various races to live together in an atmosphere of mutual respect and consideration.

28. Were the commands to the nation of Israel not to mingle with people of other nations a form of segregation?

It was a form of segregation, but it was not based on color, political aspirations, or patriotism. This separation of the Israelites from other nations was commanded by God, and had to do with His promise to Abraham that through him and his seed, all the nations of the earth would be blessed. This promise was to be fulfilled through the coming of the Messiah, and thus required the maintenance of a pure seed.

We read in Deuteronomy 7:2-4, "And when the LORD thy God shall deliver them before thee; thou shalt smite them, and utterly destroy them; thou shalt make no covenant with them, . . . neither shalt thou make marriages with them; . . . for they will turn away thy son from following me, that they may serve other gods: so will the anger of the LORD be kindled against you, and destroy thee suddenly." This was the basis of the purging of the people from foreign wives, recorded in Ezra 9 and 10, and in Nehemiah 13. These passages make no reference to the *color* of the people of those nations; it had to do with their idolatry and iniquitous practices. They were of the same color race as the Israelites.

Likewise in the New Testament, the admonition to separation from unbelievers in II Corinthians 6:14-18 is not a matter of nationality, color, or politics but of faith in Christ, or the lack of it, as the opening statement of the passage shows: "Be ye not unequally yoked together with unbelievers." This kind of separation applies to people in every walk of life who would in other respects be equals; though we may add that we should not consider "separation" in the spiritual sense to mean "isolation." We must be in contact with people to win them for Christ.

29. What was the purpose of speaking in tongues?

In the only reference to speaking in tongues in the four Gospels, it is included in a list of miraculous manifestations which were to be given as "signs," thus authenticating the gospel message as having divine authority. Moses, at Mount Sinai, did not give the law to Israel without manifestations of divine power to authenticate it. These manifestations were in keeping with the nature of the law, so that the mountain quaked, and smoked, and there were evidences of divine judgment, suggesting the character of the law and its penalties.

Since Israel had been under the law for some fifteen hundred years, it was needful that there be some divine authentication of the gospel message which was now displacing the law as the basis of man's relationship to God. In Mark 16:17-19 the Lord Jesus gives a list of such authenticating "signs," which would follow "them that believe"; and verse 20 adds, "And they went forth, and preached every where, the Lord working with them, and confirming the word with signs following."

Hebrews 2:3-4 seems to confirm this view: "How shall we escape, if we neglect so great salvation; which at the first began to be spoken by the Lord, and was confirmed unto us by them that heard him; God also bearing them witness, both with signs and wonders, and with divers miracles, and gifts of the Holy Ghost, according to his own will?" This last clause is significant, for nowhere in Scripture is it recorded that people sought the gift of tongues. The gift, whenever given, was by the sovereign act of God.

The list of signs given in Mark 16 as authentication of the gospel message is in keeping with the character of the gospel. They were powers of healing and of overcoming the adverse effects of sin. Just as the demonstrations of God's power at Sinai were in keeping with judgment, so these were in keeping with salvation. The gift of tongues is likewise suited to this context, since in this gospel dispensation the message of God was no longer to be presented only to "the house of Israel" (Matt. 10:6), but was to be preached to "every creature" (Mark 16:15).

30. Is speaking in tongues necessary to prove that one is baptized with the Spirit?

There is nothing in the Bible to say that speaking in tongues is the mark of the baptism of the Holy Spirit, though in a few cases this gift accompanied the impartation of the Holy Spirit to believers. It should be noticed that speaking in tongues is recorded historically only a few times in the Book of Acts, though it is referred to doctrinally in I Corinthians 12; 13; and 14. Since all believers are said to be baptized by (or, in) the Spirit (I Cor. 12:13), and not all believers are said to have spoken in tongues, it would seem evident that speaking in tongues was not intended to be the proof of one's having been baptized by (or, in) the Spirit.

I Corinthians 12:28-31 indicates clearly that speaking in tongues was not true of all believers, and while chapter 14 does not forbid speaking in tongues, it does definitely disparage the gift in comparison with prophesying, and nowhere in the chapter do we find a statement that the exercise of this power was required in order to be assured that we have experienced the baptism of the Holy Spirit. No mention is made in Acts of speaking in tongues except on the day of Pentecost, in the household of Cornelius, and in the case of the disciples of John the Baptist when they were brought into the full revelation of Christianity (Acts 19). However, in the case of the Samaritans in Acts 8 speaking in tongues may be implied. We believe it had special significance in these cases, and was not intended to be an abiding and universal proof of a Christian's being baptized in the Holy Spirit.

31. It is my understanding that human personality lies in man's intellectual and psychological system—his soul, and that his body gives him contact with his material surroundings. Do animals have a soul? If so, how do they differ from human beings?

Man not only has a soul (his intellectual and psychological system) and a body, which gives him contact with his material surroundings, but he has also a spirit (I Thess. 5:23). While it is often said that man's spirit gives him God-consciousness, this may be oversimplification because man in every part of his being is responsible to God. We can honor or dishonor God in every part of our being, spirit and soul and body. Mary, the mother of Jesus, in her prayer called the Magnificat said, "My soul doth magnify the Lord, and my spirit hath rejoiced in God my Saviour" (Luke 1:46-47). These verses show that both spirit and soul are involved in the worship of God, and I Corinthians 6:20 adds, "Glorify God in your body." (The balance of the verse, "and in your spirit, which are God's," is omitted in the critical texts.)

While the functions of spirit and soul and body are not specifically defined, we can get some idea of them by a simple comparison. Minerals have form and substance, but not life. They are not born; they do not die. They do not grow nor change by any inward processes, though they are subject to change by the operation of physical forces from without. Plants, though composed entirely of mineral matter, have life. At a certain time they begin to live; they grow and develop into maturity; and they die. Yet plants do not have self-consciousness. Their roots will often be extended in search of moisture, but they do not move from place to place, nor do they rear their young.

Animals, like plants, have form and substance, and also life; but they have also self-consciousness, which plants have not. One can trim a hedge without pain to the plant, but trimming a dog's ears and tail are a different matter. Animals not only are born, and mature, and die, but in the process they mate, and in many cases establish some kind of home, and enjoy some measure of family life. Animals have attachments, and antipathies too, and manifest a consciousness of persons and things around them. The Septuagint version of Genesis 1:20 speaks of God commanding the waters to bring forth creatures "of living souls." This confirms the fact that animals have a consciousness different from plant life in God's order of creation.

Man has a spirit which undoubtedly gives him certain spiritual capacities which animals do not have, yet it is not possible to give exact definition to man's soul and spirit. Ancient philosophers used to speak of man as having an "animal soul" and a "rational soul." This concept may correspond roughly to what the Bible calls soul and spirit. Man's appetites and physical desires are attributed to the soul. It is said of Shechem, the son of Hamor, the Hivite prince, that "his soul clave unto Dinah the daughter of Jacob, and he loved the damsel" (Gen. 34:3). It is not said that his *spirit* clave to Dinah in love.

The soul is taken to represent the person, as in the text, "The soul that sinneth, it shall die" (Ezek. 18:20). The context shows this refers to the person, as also in Genesis 46:26, "All the souls that came with Jacob into Egypt, which came out of his loins, besides Jacob's sons' wives, all the souls were threescore and six." We say that "a person was born," but we do not say "a body was born," nor "a spirit was born"—though both body and spirit came when the person was born. But we consider the soul to be the seat of the personality, and representative of it. Yet Proverbs 11:13 speaks of "a faithful *spirit*," and Proverbs 16:18 of "a haughty spirit." We are told in Proverbs 16:2 that "the LORD weigheth the spirits," something that is not said of the souls (or bodies) of men. From this we take it that a man's spirit is connected with his mind and will, and is intended to be the dominating factor in his life, while the soul is related more to the emotional side of his nature. But these are not absolute distinctions, and the functions of man's entire being—spirit and soul and body— are interwoven as parts of an integrated personality.

32. **Why, in view of Proverbs 22:6, do children of non-Christian parents often turn out better than the children of Christian parents? Often the children of non-Christians are well poised and successful, and children of Christian parents often are not.**

It is difficult to put human experience into categories. Physically we do not all respond equally to various medicines, or food. Emotionally and spiritually, we respond in various ways. Several factors are involved in the response of the individual.

Generally, it is a decided asset to have Christian parents. To be brought up under the Word of God is a great blessing, and gives one a foundation on which the Holy Spirit can work. Often a Scripture verse or a hymn, memorized in childhood, comes back to one's memory in a time of particular need, and proves a blessing. Also, a life ordered by the Word of God is far more satisfying than one governed by the caprice and passion of an unregenerate heart.

I do not think the scripture cited, Proverbs 22:6, guarantees the salvation of a child, though in many cases that does result. "Train up a child in the way he should go: and when he is old, he will not depart from it." This seems more a general principle than a specific promise, since conversion requires a response of faith in the heart of the child (or adult).

Regarding success, I would say that the Christian has a different standard of success than the non-Christian does. The Christian *may* prosper in earthly things, but not necessarily so. In Psalm 73 Asaph told how he envied the prosperity of wicked men until he went into the sanctuary. Then he understood their end, and realized that earthly prosperity is not the standard by which God's people are to judge the values of life. Satan may attack one who tries to live for the Lord. Also, God's children are the objects of God's chastening, to conform us to the image of Christ. Such chastening may involve loss of earthly prosperity, or even of health; but the purpose and end result is blessing. Still many Christians are eminently successful in the affairs of this life. Whether one is successful or not depends partly on God's will, and partly on the responses of the individual.

33. What does the Bible teach about children who die before reaching an age of accountability?

So far as we know, there is no direct statement in the Bible about the status of those who die in infancy or before reaching an age of accountability. We are told the basis of salvation, and the way it is made effective in the individual. On God's side, "without shedding of blood is no remission" (Heb. 9:22). There is no other basis on which He can or will forgive sins. On man's side, this becomes effective through faith in Christ, and the acknowledgment of Him as our Lord (Rom. 10:9-10).

The application of this presents no problem in the case of adults. But what about those who die before they are mentally capable of making such a decision? While Scripture does not answer directly, there are some indirect references which we believe furnish a satisfying answer. In Matthew 19:14 the Lord Jesus said, "Suffer little children, and forbid them not, to come unto me: for of such is the kingdom of heaven."

Also, in Luke 19:10, our Lord, in addressing Zacchaeus, an adult, said: "For the Son of man is come to seek and to save that which was lost." But in Matthew 18:11, where the subject of the passage is little children, He said, "The Son of man is come to save that which was lost" (the words "to seek" not being used). This comparison seems to me very significant, and, in the light of the statement in Matthew 19, I take it that those who die before reaching the mental and spiritual capability of understanding are saved by the atonement of Christ.

It should be understood, however, that this is not because of the "innocence" of the child, for Scripture plainly states, in Ephesians 2:3, that we "were by nature the children of wrath, even as others." No one is innocent, and many scriptures teach that all men need to be saved. In the case of a person reaching an age of accountability, he must accept Christ by faith (John 1:12-13) in order to be saved. But we take it that a person who dies before reaching the stage of development where he is capable of doing this is accepted by God because the death of Christ avails for him.

34. Does Hebrews 4:12 mean that a person receives a spirit at new birth?

The verse says: "For the word of God is quick [living] and powerful, and sharper than any twoedged sword, piercing even to the dividing asunder of soul and spirit, and of the joints and marrow, and is a discerner of the thoughts and intents of the heart." This does not speak of imparting a spirit to man, but makes a distinction between spirit and soul. The language is obviously metaphorical, as can be seen from the reference to "the joints and marrow."

On this text Vincent says, in his *Word Studies*, "The form of expression is poetical, and signifies that the word penetrates to the inmost recesses of our spiritual being as a sword cuts through the joints and marrow of the body. The separation is not of one part from another, but operates in each department of the spiritual nature. The expression is expanded and defined by the next clause." The clause which follows is: "and is a discerner of the thoughts and intents of the heart."

From this text it seems clear to me that God's Word brings to light and emphasizes certain distinctions which men are inclined to overlook. However, I do not see any suggestion that God imparts a spirit at the time of a man's new birth, for the spirit is an integral part of man's being when he is born into the world.

35. In what sense do believers have "eternal life" if everyone is going to live forever?

When God created animal life, He did so by the word of His power. But when God created man, "God . . . breathed into his nostrils the breath of life; and man became a living soul" (Gen. 2:7). That is to say, God communicated something to man which He did not communicate to animals. The word "breath" can be taken to mean "spirit." So, while man "became a living soul," it was as one possessing a spirit, without which the body is dead, we are told in James 2:26. The fact that this spirit came directly from God indicates that God communicated something of Himself to man, and this gave man endless being. This remains true of man, whether he is ever saved or not.

The fact that all men live forever was clearly stated by the Lord Jesus Christ in Luke 20:37-38, where He pointed out that when God spoke to Moses at the burning bush, He called Himself the God of Abraham, and the God of Isaac, and the God of

Jacob. "He is not a God of the dead," the Lord Jesus said, "but of the living: for all live unto him." Many scriptures make it clear that all of the human race have endless being. In Luke 16 the Lord Jesus showed that those who die in their sins, as well as those who are saved, continue to exist after their life on this earth ends.

But the term "eternal life" is used only of believers, because this is the very life of God Himself (Eph. 4:18). This life is communicated to believers in Christ through the new birth, as we are told in John 1:12-13. When a person is born of God through faith in Christ, he is given the right to be called a child of God. Had Adam and Eve never sinned they would have lived endlessly, but they would not have possessed the life of God. They had creature life. After they sinned, they still would have existed endlessly, but apart from God. Through Christ's redemption, when we believe in Christ His life is communicated to us, so that we have God's own "eternal life." It is not only endless existence but the very life of God, giving us capacity to be in His presence. In the marginal reading of I Timothy 6:19 this is called "what is really life."

36. Are Roman Catholics right in saying that Peter was the first pope, and that all succeeding popes represent Christ?

Usually this claim is based on what Christ said to Peter in Matthew 16:18: "And I say also unto thee, That thou art Peter, and upon this rock I will build my church; and the gates of hell shall not prevail against it." It is claimed that Peter is the rock on which the church is built, and that his primacy is passed on to successors elected by the college of cardinals.

I believe there are several fallacies in this reasoning. Peter did not consider himself the rock on which the church is built, but in his first epistle he spoke of Christ as a chief cornerstone, chosen of God (I Peter 2:4-7). The Apostle Paul emphatically taught that men could lay no other foundation than Jesus Christ (I Cor. 3:11). And whatever meaning we attach to John 20:23, these words about forgiving sins were spoken not to Peter alone but to the ten who were present. (Thomas was absent, and Judas had left the group.)

In no place in Scripture is there any indication that any one person was the appointed leader of the church, and after chapter 15 of Acts, there is no other mention of Peter in Scripture except for his two epistles and the historical mention of him in Paul's letter to the Galatians. Instead of Peter, it was Paul who from that time received the greatest prominence. But Paul disclaims any official priority, and nothing in the biblical record, including Peter's own epistles, gives any suggestion that he was the official leader. At the conference in Acts 15 it was James, the Lord's brother, who took the lead. And there is no biblical instruction for the choosing of any successor.

37. Could those who are called apostates have been born-again Christians; or did they just have that outward appearance?

The word *apostate* requires definition, since it is not a biblical word, although the noun "apostasy" occurs twice (Acts 21:21 and II Thess. 2:3). The first of these speaks of "apostasy from Moses," which we take to mean departure from what one formerly professed as truth. According to my understanding of the word, an *apostate* is one who, having professed to receive Jesus Christ as Lord and Saviour, later renounces Christ and Christianity; and I take it that such a person is not truly saved. In fact, when a person who has understanding of what is involved purposefully renounces Christ, it is a question whether such a person can be renewed unto repentance (Heb. 6:4-8; 10:26-31).

There may be an illustration of this in the parable of the sower and the seed. In Mark 4:16-17, where we read the Lord Jesus' explanation of that part of the parable which relates to the seed which fell on stony ground, He said: "And these are they . . . who, when they have heard the word, immediately receive it with gladness; and have no root in themselves, and so endure but for a time: afterward, when affliction or persecution ariseth for the word's sake, immediately they are offended [or, stumbled]."

In the parable this seed sprang up and showed every sign of life, but it was found later that the seed had not become rooted in the ground. All the signs of life came from the seed, through the medium of the ground, but without becoming rooted in the ground. "These . . . have no root in themselves." An apostate therefore would be a person who receives the Word of God, and seems to bear fruit, but the root of the matter is not in him, and later on he renounces his former profession of faith.

We do not believe a person born again through faith in Christ can later be lost.* It is significant that in Matthew 7:23 the Lord Jesus will say to those shut out of the kingdom, "I *never knew you.*" He will not say, "I knew you once, but not any longer." They had professed to know Him, but He never knew them. This lends significance to the remark by the Apostle Paul in Galatians 4:9: "But now, after that ye have known God, or rather are known of God, . . ." The important thing is for a person to be sure he is known by Christ as a true believer. Such a person will not become an apostate. In Luke 10:20 the Lord Jesus said to His disciples, "Rejoice, because your names are written in heaven." Was this to awaken in Judas an awareness that his name was not written in heaven? He is, in my understanding, an example of apostasy.

38. Is cremation wrong for Christians?

We do not know of any precept telling how to dispose of the body when a person dies, but the universal example in the Bible is burial. This suggests not only respect for the body as an integral part of the person but is an implied acknowledgment of resurrection. We might compare the expressions found in I Corinthians 15, "It is sown . . . it is raised." But burial is not commanded, and we can think of some good reasons why it should not be.

If the Bible commanded burial, serious questions might be raised concerning anyone who did not have a proper burial; for

*See our discussion of this subject under question 142.

instance, martyrs burned at the stake. Sometimes persons have decreed that their bodies be burned after death in the belief this would prevent resurrection, in the hope of escaping the judgment of God. A little serious reflection will show the folly of this. If God is able to raise the dead at all, He certainly can as easily raise one whose body was burned as one whose body had decayed in a grave.

But, while not giving direct instructions, the Bible does teach respect for the body and the resurrection, in a future day, of all who die. Lack of proper burial, when willful, indicates lack of respect for the person. Sometimes cremation is practiced for reasons which involve neither desecration of the body nor an attempt to evade the judgment of God. I do not know of any scripture which is violated in such cases.

39. Does possessing the "crown of life," mentioned in both James and the Revelation, mean the same thing as possessing eternal life?

No, the "crown of life" in each case is mentioned as a reward. In James 1:12 it is promised for faithful living: "Blessed is the man that endureth temptation: for when he is tried, he shall receive the crown of life, which the Lord hath promised to them that love him." In this chapter the Apostle James refers to two kinds of temptation—the temptations or testings which come from God and the temptations to do evil, which come from Satan or from our own sinful nature within us. We are to welcome the first kind of temptation and shun the other kind.

The various testings which God sends develop Christian character. We read, in Genesis 22:1, that the Lord "tempted Abraham." God "tested" his willingness to sacrifice for Him. Abraham's response strengthened his resolution, while God's dealing with him on that occasion resulted in great joy and a deeper realization of the wisdom, love, and power of God. It is as we endure that God is glorified; and the word *endure* also implies that we gain inner strength. The reward is "the crown of life, which the Lord hath promised to them that love him." It is not life itself, which the believer already has.

In Revelation 2:10 the crown of life is promised to those who are "faithful unto death." We take this to mean those who lay down their lives as martyrs for Christ. It is interesting to see that this reward can be gained either by faithful living, as in the case of the Apostle Paul, or by a martyr's death, as in the case of John the Baptist. I might add, however, that I believe both these men won the crown both ways.

40. Is the death of a believer to be considered the second coming of Christ for us?

So far as I know, the death of a believer does not speak of Christ coming for us but of our going to be with Him. Paul said, in Philippians 1:23, that "to depart and be with Christ, . . . is far better"; and in II Corinthians 5:8 he spoke of being "absent from the body, and . . . present [or at home] with the Lord." In both these verses the thought is not that of Christ coming for us but our going to be with Him.

We read, in Luke 16, about the death of Lazarus, the beggar, and how the angels carried him to Abraham's bosom. But there is no suggestion that Abraham came for Lazarus.

Perhaps the nearest approach to this idea is found in the account of the death of Stephen, the first Christian martyr. Stephen saw "Jesus standing on the right hand of God." This implies that our Lord rose up to receive Stephen—a high honor, but He did not come for him.

There are two aspects to the second coming of Christ, but neither relates to the death of the believer. In fact, when Christ comes for us, those then living will not die at all (I Cor. 15:51; I Thess. 4:17). The second coming of Christ is His personal advent, whether at the first resurrection, or when He comes to establish His kingdom on earth.

(See also the answer to question 112.)

41. How could the foolish virgins, referred to in the parable in Matthew 25, buy oil?

This reference to buying oil is, of course, a figure of speech. We find something similar in Isaiah 55:1: "Ho, every one that thirsteth, come ye to the waters, and he that hath no money; come ye, buy, and eat; yea, come, buy wine and milk without money and without price." The language is all figurative, but the basic point is clear. In a purchase, we make a thing our own, and the Israelites were here admonished by the prophet to take possession of the true values of life. And while these values may be ours "without money and without price," yet to possess them often involves turning from what we are doing.

The Lord Jesus used a similar figure in Revelation 3:17-18: "Because thou sayest, I am rich, and increased with goods, and have need of nothing; and knowest not that thou art wretched, and miserable, and poor, and blind, and naked: I counsel thee to buy of me gold tried in the fire that thou mayest be rich; and white raiment, that thou mayest be clothed, and that the shame of thy nakedness do not appear. . . ."

The mistake of the foolish virgins was to expect the wise virgins to give them some of their oil. The wise virgins rightly replied, "Go ye rather to them that sell, and buy for yourselves." The force of these words, applied to us, is that each of us must have direct dealing with God. We cannot receive His grace from any other source.

42. Does Matthew 7:1 ("Judge not, that ye be not judged") mean that we are not to distinguish between those who are saved and those who are lost?

No, because there are numerous other scriptures which teach that we must make such a distinction. For example, II Corinthians 6:14: "Be ye not unequally yoked together with unbelievers."

Christ, in Matthew 7:1, was speaking of our having a censorious spirit toward others, judging their motives, which we have no capacity to judge. If I am constantly finding fault with others, in all likelihood it is I who am at fault. Criticizing others is one of the forms of self-gratification. We despise a person who boasts, perhaps because of envy, when we have nothing to boast of. But we make up for our deficiency by discrediting and disparaging others to make them appear less worthy than ourselves. Of the two, judging is more despicable than boasting, though both are wrong.

Likewise, the judging of people's motives is wrong. We can guess, but often such guessing is based on what our motives would be in a similar situation. Because our guesses are often totally wrong, we do the person an injustice which is almost impossible to correct. Our Lord condemns such judging.

But in the matter of salvation, while God is the final judge, ordinarily it is not too difficult to distinguish between the saved and the lost. A saved person is a believer in Christ, one who acknowledges Him as Lord and Saviour. An unsaved person does not believe in Christ, and has not submitted to Him in faith. Where people are clear in their profession of faith or unbelief, there is no problem. The Bible also indicates that with conversion comes new birth, resulting in a change of life. This is an alternative basis for judging the genuineness of a person's profession of faith in Christ. When no evidence of such a change of life is seen in a person, one may well wonder about the validity of his verbal profession.

At best our judgment is fallible, and there may be cases such as that of Simon Magus, recorded in Acts 8. He was accepted as a believer, on his profession of faith, and was baptized along with others. His later conduct showed plainly that he had "neither part nor lot in this matter" (v. 21), and so he was rejected.

We deal with people on the basis of their profession of faith in Christ, backed up by godly living, recognizing that their final destiny rests with God, and not with us.

43. In Matthew 25 we are told of the judgment of the nations. How can nations be judged?

There is a sense in which nations can be judged, though I do not think that is what is referred to in Matthew 25. God allows nations to reap what they sow. Though He used the Babylonians to chastise His people Israel, He later dealt with Babylon because they, on their part, had acted with hatred and cruelty. We find in history many examples of nations who suffered after having committed crimes against others. Scripture indicates that God providentially orders and arranges such retribution.

In Matthew 25, where "all nations" are described as being gathered before the Lord for judgment, the results of that judgment are "everlasting punishment" and "life eternal" (v. 46). These expressions, it seems to me, preclude mass judgment of the nations. Many have thought that nations which will be friendly to believers during the Tribulation will enter into the millennium, while those who are not friendly will be destroyed. Prophecy does not indicate that any nation on earth at that period will be friendly to believers.

We cannot even be certain that all mankind will be gathered before the Lord. Some think that Isaiah 66:18-20 has application here. In this view, the Lord will gather before Him all those from the nations who have participated in Armageddon, and who will be present in the land of Palestine at that time. These will be judged on the basis of their relationship to Christ, expressed in their treatment of His "brethren." These "brethren" are probably chiefly the believing remnant of Israel, but would include other believers as well.

After the separation of the sheep from the goats (among these nations) the Lord will then send messengers "unto the [rest of the] nations, . . . afar off, that have not heard my fame, neither have seen my glory; and they shall declare my glory among the Gentiles" (Isa. 66:19). It will then be left for these to accept or reject the message given them, and the Lord's dealing with them will be based on this. It is impossible to give authoritative details, and it is doubtful if God meant that we should understand things in the detail in which they will be seen at that time. The same was true prior to His first advent. Things became apparent after His advent which had not been understood before.

We may say in general that God deals with peoples nationally in a providential way. He also deals with individuals providentially, but His eternal judgments will be based on the individual's relationship to Christ. It appears that Christ will not be dealing with men providentially as He sets up His millennial kingdom, but on the basis of a personal profession of faith in Him, as indicated in Matthew 18:3.

44. Does the term "bride of Christ" include only New Testament believers, that is, those saved after Pentecost?

It is our understanding that this is so, and that the Church is not simply a continuation of the nation of Israel on a spiritual plane. The promise made to Abraham involved physical offspring, although faith was required on their part for them to share Abraham's blessing. The later promises of God to Israel had to do with the birth of the Messiah, who (according to the flesh) would be a descendant of Abraham, Isaac, Jacob, and David. Many of the promises made to Israel were earthly, and sufficiently specific, with geographical locations, to make it impossible to spiritualize these without doing violence to the text. They promised a future glory on earth which has not yet been fulfilled. To deny a future fulfillment would be to nullify a large part of Scripture. On the other hand, such a fulfillment fits in easily with New Testament prophecies of Christ's second coming to the earth.

In Matthew 16:18 the Lord Jesus spoke of the Church as a fresh, divine revelation; but He placed its beginning in the future. Up to the time of His death, the Temple and its ritual were not completely disowned of God, but when He died, the veil of the Temple was rent in twain from top to bottom. In the light of Hebrews 9:6-10, we take it that at that time God did set aside the Temple ritual which He had ordained in the days of Moses.

Since the Church is the "body of Christ" (Eph. 1:22-23) which is formed by the baptism of the Holy Spirit (I Cor. 12:13), we take it that it was not formed until the Holy Spirit was given at Pentecost (Acts 1:5 and chapter 2). The indwelling of believers by the Holy Spirit brought them into an association with Christ (Eph. 5:30) and with each other (Rom. 12:4-5) which is not predicated of believers of any other dispensation. Ephesians 5:25-33 identifies the bride of Christ with this spiritual body.

It seems clear to me, from the passages referred to, that only those who believe in Christ during this church dispensation are said to be members of the body and bride of Christ.

45. What is meant by the expression "try the spirits" in I John 4:1? To do this, does a person need to possess the special gift mentioned in I Corinthians 12:10?

I John 4:1 is an exhortation: "Beloved, believe not every spirit, but try the spirits whether they are of God: because many false prophets are gone out into the world." From the latter part of the verse we gather that the *spirits* referred to are not essentially spirit beings but rather the spirit which animates the person. Does the person speak by the Spirit of God, or is he one who speaks "from himself"? That such an one might be controlled by an evil spirit is easily possible, though that is not necessarily implied. We speak of a person having a "gentle spirit," or a "hasty spirit," and we do not mean "spirit possession."

While the gift of "discerning of spirits" mentioned in I Corinthians 12:10 would no doubt help, all Christians are here exhorted not to believe every spirit but to "try" the spirits. There are two means of doing this. One is given in verse 2: "Every spirit that confesseth that Jesus Christ is come in the flesh is of God." Those who deny that Jesus Christ came in the flesh are not of God. The form of statement implies the recognition of Jesus Christ as the incarnate Son of God.

The other test is given in verse 6: "We are of God: he that knoweth God heareth us; he that is not of God heareth not us." This, I take it, refers to the inspired Scriptures. Those who are "of God" acknowledge the inspired Scriptures as the authoritative revelation of God. Hence the tests which any child of God can apply to anyone who professes to represent Him are these: Does he accept the truth concerning Christ's person? Does he accept the authority of the Bible?

46. What is the meaning of "castaway"' in I Corinthians 9:27?

In this verse Paul wrote: "I keep under my body, and bring it into subjection: lest that by any means, when I have preached to others, I myself should be a castaway." The word *castaway* is better translated "rejected" or "disapproved." Some have taken what Paul said here to mean that he feared his soul might be lost at the end, but the word used does not necessarily mean this, nor is that the subject of the passage.

In the preceding verses Paul was urging the Corinthian believers to live in such a way that they would merit a prize or reward in the day of Christ. In verse 26 he told them that he was practicing what he preached, and he added in verse 27, "I keep under my body." Vincent says this is "a feeble translation, . . . missing the metaphor. The word means *to strike under the eye; to give one a black eye.*" The verb occurs only twice in the New Testament.

Paul's earnest effort to keep his body under control was not because he feared that his soul would be lost, for the salvation of one's soul is secured by the atoning blood of Christ. Rather, he made his body his slave, instead of allowing himself to be a slave to its passions. In this way he could use his physical strength in the service of Christ, and so at Christ's *bema* (judgment seat) he would not stand disapproved, but receive a reward.

47. Did Christ ascend into heaven twice, once privately, as mentioned in John 20:17, and once publicly forty days later from Mount Olivet? Does not Christ's invitation to His disciples to handle Him (Luke 24:39) show that He had ascended to heaven since He had spoken to Mary?

This is often taught, with the claim that He had to ascend after

His resurrection to present His blood to His Father. In my opinion this teaching is erroneous. I believe that Christ's blood was efficacious as soon as it was shed, as the rending of the veil showed. His resurrection was proof that God had accepted the offering of Himself for our sins. In Hebrews 9:12 we read concerning Christ, "Neither by the blood of goats and calves, but by his own blood he entered in once into the holy place, having obtained eternal redemption for us." His entrance was because He had obtained eternal redemption, not to effect it.

Perhaps we misunderstand our Lord's words to Mary: "Touch me not; for I am not yet ascended to my Father. . . ." These words are more literally rendered, "Do not cling to me" (Berkeley version, and others). He did not mean He was not to be touched but that He would not return to the former relationship. He must ascend to the Father, and assume a new relationship to His disciples. Paul wrote of this in II Corinthians 5:16, "Henceforth know we no man after the flesh: yea, though we have known Christ after the flesh, yet now henceforth know we him no more."

Mary had to learn she could not continue clinging to Christ in the flesh. She must learn to know Him now as glorified—He was on His way to ascension into heaven. During our Lord's lifetime, the Apostle John had laid his head on Jesus' bosom, but when he saw the Lord in His glorified state, according to Revelation 1, John "fell at his feet as dead." The disciples' personal relationship with Christ while He was on earth was a temporary relationship, never to be resumed.

The incident related in Luke 24:39 was in an entirely different setting. There the disciples were so far from trying to reestablish the old relationship that Christ had to convince them that He was the very same Person who had died on the cross, and was now resurrected. Hence He said, "Behold, my hands and my feet, that it is I, myself: handle me, and see." This word *handle* has more the force of "touch." They were to feel His flesh, and know that He was a real Person in their midst.

48. Does the Bible allow for the possibility of a race of beings comparable to men on other planets?

We believe not, for various reasons, though I know of no direct statement on the subject. Some have thought that the very existence of so vast a universe demands that God use some of the other planets as habitations for creatures comparable to man, but they may very well serve other purposes, which it is not necessary for us to understand. There are many things in this world the usefulness of which we do not understand.

The earth is singled out in the reference in Genesis 1:1 to the creation of the universe. In my opinion this is because the Bible concerns itself with this earth and its inhabitants. There is a statement in Isaiah 45:18 which seems to confirm the thought that the earth has a unique place in God's counsels. There the prophet, speaking of God as Creator of both heavens and earth, said of the earth, "He formed it to be inhabited." So far as I know, this is said of no other planet. In Psalm 115:16 we read, "The heaven, even the heavens, are the LORD's: but the earth hath he given to the children of men." There is no suggestion that He has created other races of beings on other planets comparable to mankind.

Theological difficulties are involved in the idea of races other than mankind. Man was created in the image and likeness of God (Gen. 1:26-27). This involves also the endless existence of each human being; and God, having foreseen man's fall into sin, planned his redemption through the incarnation and atoning death of His Son. If there were another race which did not sin, why should God create men whose redemption required the sufferings and death of His Son? And if such a race exists, and they did sin, has God provided redemption for them? Has Christ taken into His being the natures of others besides men? We are told in I Timothy 2:5 that "there is one God, and one mediator between God and men, the man Christ Jesus." This verse, it seems to me, precludes the idea of His having assumed the nature of any other order of beings. Hebrews 2:16 assures us that He did not assume the nature of angels, and implies He has assumed only the nature of humanity. Speculation as to any similar order of beings seems to me to be without any biblical foundation.

49. Could the "other sheep" of John 10:16 be people on other planets, and could the ministry of angels mentioned in the Bible relate to the activities of such beings?

This question illustrates the need for interpreting Scripture by other passages of Scripture, and not by pure speculation. In the first part of this chapter the Lord Jesus had been speaking of His ministry to Israel under the figure of the "fold," and He spoke of believers in Him as being His sheep. When He spoke about having "other sheep" He was speaking of others who would believe on Him; and when He added, "who are not of this fold," quite evidently He was saying they were of nations other than Israel. In other words, He was speaking of the fact that He knew of Gentiles who would become believers.

What follows in this verse is equally conclusive in identifying these "other sheep," for Christ said, "Them also I must bring, and they shall hear my voice; and there shall be one fold, and one shepherd." A more accurate rendering would be: "so there will be one flock, one shepherd." It is not that the Gentile believers would be brought into the Jewish fold, for He had already said in verse 3 that He was leading His own sheep out of that fold. But he is saying in verse 16 that He would unite believers in Him, whether Jew or Gentile, into one new flock, of which He would Himself be the Shepherd. He is not speaking of going to other planets, but to other sheep on this planet. If there were beings on other planets they could not be united to us either as being "in Adam" or "in Christ," so this could not be the meaning of our Lord's words.

Except for fallen angels or demons, the activity of angels mentioned in the Bible is always in the service of God, and usually *on behalf of* men. However, the activity of fallen angels and demons is directed *toward* men, with no suggestion of which I am aware that they inhabit other planets, or that in their nature they are comparable to mankind.

50. Please explain the cursing of the fig tree in Mark 11. Why did Jesus put a curse on the fig tree, when the time for figs was not yet?

Let us consider first the natural circumstances involved, and then their spiritual meaning. Since "the time of figs was not yet," no fruit could have been expected on any of the trees. But as the Lord Jesus and His disciples were returning to Jerusalem, after having spent the night in Bethany, they saw "a fig tree afar off having leaves" (Mark 11:12). The marginal reading of Matthew 21:19 (lit. "a solitary fig tree") makes it clear that this one stood alone, as is evidenced also in that it was noticeable from "afar off."

This, then, was a tree which stood out from the rest because it had leaves when the others had none. A characteristic of the fig tree is that it has a form of fruit as soon as the leaves appear, so it was a proper expectation that this tree should have had fruit even though it was not yet the time of figs. Since there were leaves, there should have been fruit. But when Christ and His disciples came, they found none; and He saw fit to put a curse upon the tree.

Many expositors take a low view of this act, because they see no spiritual meaning in it. They assume it was an act of resentment, but this puts the Lord of glory on a very low plane of purely human feeling. Christ had already proved abundantly that He was not governed by feelings of hunger, as when He rejected Satan's temptation to change stones into bread when He was hungry. He experienced hunger, but He told Satan, "Man shall not live by bread alone, but by every word that proceedeth out of the mouth of God."

Such a view is an insult to Christ. And we might ask what would be the point of recording the incident at all if it did not have a spiritual significance? Often in Scripture a tree stands for a kingdom, and Israel is variously represented by the vine, the fig tree, and the olive tree. We read in Luke 21:29-31: "Behold the fig tree, and all the trees; when they now shoot forth, ye see and know of your own selves that summer is now nigh at hand.

So likewise ye, when ye see these things come to pass, know ye that the kingdom of God is nigh at hand."

The fig tree represents Israel in the aspect of a political entity, subject to God and, therefore, in a sense, God's kingdom on earth. At Christ's advent that nation, alone among all the nations, made the profession of being subject to the law of God and, therefore, representing His government on earth. Yet when Christ came to Israel, He found no fruit on that tree nationally, though there were individuals who received Him in faith as their Messiah. However, the nation was "cursed," which does not signify damnation but the judgment of God which led to their dispersion and loss of their national status. The words "for ever" are, literally, "unto the age." This implies that God will not again recognize Israel as His chosen people until the second advent of Christ.

51. How do we know there is an existence after death?

We are shut up to divine revelation (I Cor. 2:9-10) as the source of our knowledge of a world which we cannot perceive with our senses. We know there is an existence after death because such existence was revealed to men by the Son of God while He was on earth, and it is revealed to us in the Bible, the Word of God (Luke 16:19-31; 20:37-38).

The Bible tells us that God has set eternity in men's hearts (Eccl. 3:11, marginal reading). This is confirmed by the fact that men universally have a concept of life in another world. Such a life is required to give any meaning and value to life on this earth. If men died like beasts with no future life, there would be no reason to aspire to moral or spiritual values.

The Word of God tells us that there is a law of compensation in life. "Be not deceived; God is not mocked: for whatsoever a man soweth, that shall he also reap" (Gal. 6:7). I Timothy 5:24-25 indicates that whether this is realized partially in this life or not, in eternity there will be the full recompense for our lives, whether good or bad. This is necessary if we are to maintain the ultimate victory of justice, without which God would not be the Ruler and the universe itself would be headed for chaos, particularly in the area of human relations.

CHRISTIAN ETHICS

52. Does the Bible teach birth control?

To make the question more specific, I quote from a letter which said: "I am soon to be married. One friend who has ten children says God knows what is best for us, and we should accept whatever He appoints. Others say we should limit the number of children we have to what we can properly support, and not bring large families into the world who may have to suffer privation, and perhaps not be able to obtain higher education. Some have said the only birth control permissible is to abstain from sexual relations."

In the beginning God ordained that there should be two sexes, that men and women should mate in the marriage relationship, and that in this union they should bring forth children. His command was, "Be fruitful, and multiply, and replenish the earth, and subdue it" (Gen. 1:28). The word translated "replenish" does not have the meaning of "refill," which we usually give to the English word, but simply means "to fill." This command was given when Adam and Eve were the only humans on earth. This scripture does not say what men and women were to do when the earth would become so heavily populated that it would not be possible to supply food for the sustenance of the inhabitants of the earth.

Any answer given to the question asked should be relevant not only to those who live in a land of plenty but also to those who live in areas of poverty and starvation. An answer to this question also involves a discussion of whether the bringing forth of children is the only purpose of the marriage relationship. Several things militate against the view that the sole purpose of marriage is procreation of humanity. Sometimes a married couple remain barren, even though maintaining regular sexual intercourse with no effort to avoid conception. The Bible does not suggest that in this case sexual intercourse should cease.

One of the reasons given for marriage, in I Corinthians 7, is to satisfy sexual passion, and so avoid the sin of fornication. The Bible does not condone the sexual act out of wedlock, as many do today. Where marriage is not possible, each person is required to "possess his vessel in sanctification and honor" (I Thess. 4:4). But it cannot be considered sinful for married persons to have sexual intercourse apart from the express purpose and expectation of bearing children.

Limiting families has not been considered immoral by Christians generally. Even the Roman Catholic Church, whose views on the subject have been emphatic, has for years permitted its members to control the size of their families by what is called the "rhythm" method. If birth control were essentially immoral, then any method would be so. But it has become a question of method rather than of morals.

It becomes a question concerning the wisdom of practicing birth control. In the early years of human experience, in an agrarian economy, large families could help with the work. And in primitive life, young men might be called upon to guard a household from attack, whether by man or beast. Psalm 127:3 seems to refer to this. But such conditions no longer prevail in many areas of the earth.

However, many parents who have brought forth large families would testify that even though they were not able to supply them with luxuries, God has in various ways provided for their needs. Usually, even where maintaining the family and supplying its needs means a heavy burden of care, most parents are unwilling to give any of their children up for adoption, even by well-to-do relatives. They consider their children a "trust" and a "treasure." Many of the great persons of the earth have been younger children in large families. John Wesley's godly and capable mother was the twenty-fifth child of her family, and she bore her husband nineteen children. Of these John Wesley was the fifteenth, and his brother Charles, the hymn-writer, was the last. Benjamin

Franklin's father had seventeen children, and Benjamin was the fifteenth child, the youngest of the sons.

It is not always an asset to be born and reared in an atmosphere of luxury and advantage. God providentially cares for large families, and while they may lack certain environmental advantages, they often gain inward moral and spiritual values which others lack. Children in large families are more likely to become self-reliant and develop to a higher degree those personal capabilities with which God has endowed them. There is the danger that we shall adopt a false standard of social values which places undue emphasis on advantages.

I have been discussing the use of birth control by people who are properly and lawfully married in the sight of God and man, but it must be said that it is never right to practice birth control in order to commit immoral acts. To use contraceptives to prevent the natural consequences of sinful intercourse is only adding to the sin.

53. Is divorce permissible where one partner has committed adultery? Is it mandatory?

The circumstances giving rise to this question were that the husband had fallen into bad company, and was practicing adultery. The wife discovered it; and the husband confessed his sin, and repented of it, and forsook it. The wife forgave him, and the marriage was reestablished, but she wondered if she were disobeying Scripture in so doing.

Many conflicting views are held about the subject of divorce, indicating that in this area of Bible study, as in others, we require the guidance of the Holy Spirit to understand both the meaning of Scripture and its application to our lives. God's mind must be "spiritually discerned" (I Cor. 2:14). Some persons understand our Lord to be teaching, in Matthew 19, that divorce is not permitted to Christians under any circumstances. But the statement in verse 9, "except it be for fornication," seems to me, as to many others, an intended exception to the rule.

Many have insisted that the term *fornication* refers only to sexual intercourse before marriage, and not to adultery afterward, but we believe that while the word *adultery* applies properly only where at least one of the parties involved is married, the word *fornication* is a more general term and applies to any unlawful sexual intercourse. Others, while recognizing this meaning, attempt to discredit the statement in Matthew because it is not repeated in similar passages elsewhere in the New Testament. This, however, would be a very precarious basis on which to reject an otherwise authenticated text.

Now as to divorce being mandatory where one partner is guilty of adultery, we believe the whole of Scripture, as well as God's dealings with us, shows that this is not an unpardonable sin. Normally, marriage is intended to last "so long as ye both shall live," and Romans 7:1-3 shows that the death of one of the partners is what properly breaks the tie. Various scriptures show that we honor God most by maintaining the marriage relationship so long as it is possible to do so, even in the face of abuses.

It is well to keep in mind this principle of God: "He that covereth his sins shall not prosper; but whoso confesseth and forsaketh them shall have mercy" (Prov. 28:13). We believe this applies in the field of human relationships also, and mercy should be shown by those who have themselves experienced the mercy of God in the forgiveness of their own sins. But sometimes the guilty party does not repent, and in some cases an intolerable situation arises where divorce becomes the only acceptable course of action, distasteful though it may be. But forgiveness, where circumstances permit, should be granted. Our Lord spoke a special parable to teach such forgiveness in Matthew 18:21-35.

54. Is remarriage after divorce ever permissible?

There are those who consider Romans 7:1-3 to be conclusively against remarriage after divorce. But in my opinion they misinterpret the passage. In this passage divorce is not under consideration. The normal state of marriage is used to illustrate the obligation of those who were under the law. It was in force until terminated by death. People are married so long as both live. When one dies, the bond is broken, and the other is free to marry another if he so desires. The breaking of the bond of the law was accomplished, not because the law died, but because we died to it. Verse 6 should read, "Now we are delivered from the law, having died to that wherein we were held." We are now married to Christ in newness of life, through the new birth. Divorce is not under consideration in this passage.

In my understanding of the Bible, a divorce obtained on scriptural grounds breaks the marriage tie. In Deuteronomy 24:1-4 we find the Old Testament law of divorce. Referring to this, the Lord Jesus said, in Matthew 19:8, "Moses because of the hardness of your hearts suffered you to put away your wives: but from the beginning it was not so." In this passage, Christ limited the ground for divorce to the single cause of unfaithfulness but, so far as I can see, He did not change the nature or meaning of divorce itself.

Deuteronomy 24:2 shows that a divorced person (we are presuming the divorce to be scripturally obtained) is free to remarry. In fact, in this case it is the guilty party who is referred to. Without debating the ramifications of this, it seems clear that divorce means the breaking of the marriage tie in the sight of God. Where divorce is obtained by human law, but contrary to God's laws, remarriage after divorce can well mean legalized adultery, which God cannot countenance.

55. How does church discipline fit in with the text, "Judge not, that ye be not judged"?

We have discussed elsewhere the meaning of this text. (See question 42.)

Church discipline is a matter not of personalities but of the testimony of Christ through His people corporately. The Church is declared in the Bible to be the "body of Christ," and is called, in I Timothy 3:15, "the pillar and ground of truth." When the conduct of a member of the church becomes a public scandal, the person cannot retain his standing in the Christian community.

I Corinthians 5 gives an example of a man in the church at Corinth who fell into gross sin. The Corinthians, ignoring the shame of this, were boasting about the gifts and attainments of various people in the church. Paul told them they should have been humbled, and should have asked God to remove this blot from their testimony. The case was evidently one that had received wide publicity, since Paul heard about it when he was in another country.

Paul instructed the church at Corinth to expel such a person from their membership, and to do the same with others whose lives were openly sinful. He did not recommend eliminating the exercise of mercy and forgiveness where the circumstances might warrant this, and even in the case of this grossly sinful man, Paul later, after the man showed repentance, recommended his restoration (II Cor. 2:6-9).

The Lord Jesus showed, in Matthew 18, how a purely personal matter might become sufficiently serious to bring it before the whole assembly. He also showed that the matter, before it was ended, might require church discipline. Such discipline is not a matter of vindicating one person and condemning another but of maintaining a moral and spiritual state in the assembly in which the Holy Spirit can work ungrieved and unquenched.

56. Is not capital punishment a violation of the New Testament commandment to love one another?

The character of God never changes. It is a false concept that in the Old Testament God is revealed as a vengeful God, but in the New Testament, as a God of love. The righteousness and love of God are expressed in different ways at different times, but His nature does not change. Both characteristics were always part of His nature and being.

We must distinguish between God's instructions to individuals in their personal relationships and His instructions concerning human government for the preservation of an ordered society in a world of sin. When man was governed by conscience alone, before the flood, we read that violence and corruption filled the earth (Gen. 6). God brought the flood upon men as a judgment, preserving Noah and his family. After the flood God ordained human government as a bolster for man's conscience, and His command was, "Whoso sheddeth man's blood, by man shall his blood be shed" (Gen. 9:6).

The New Testament does not nullify this. In Romans 13 we read that the representative of human government is "the minister of God, a revenger to execute wrath upon him that doeth evil" (v. 4). The same verse states, "He beareth not the sword in vain." A sword is not used for writing traffic tickets. It is speaking of executing judgment on evildoers, and we believe this includes capital punishment, where this is indicated by the nature of the crime committed.

In our personal dealings one with another we are to practice love and forbearance, but to act in this way toward criminals, and especially murderers, would soon result in a disordered and violent society. While sociologists often proclaim the opposite, crime statistics show an alarming increase of violent crimes where just penalties are not executed upon criminals.

57. What should be my response as a Christian to my boss, who requires me to lie for him? Sometimes he asks me to say he is not there when he is. Sometimes he dictates letters stating things I know are not true.

Christian conduct must be the response of the individual to the claims of Christ. It is only as we act in the conviction we are doing His will and pleasing Him that we can count on Him to keep us, and open His way before us. Besides the Old Testament commandment not to bear false witness (Exodus 20:16), which includes "speaking lies" (Prov. 6:19), the Lord Jesus declared, in John 8:44, that Satan is "a liar and the father of it." Many other scriptures forbid lying and command us to speak the truth, besides those which tell us to do all things in the Name of the Lord Jesus and for the glory of God.

In view of these scriptures I would say that a Christian is justified in telling his (or her) boss that he cannot conscientiously lie, and then refuse to do so. If this means the loss of the job, the Christian can count on the Lord to make some other provision which will not require dishonesty. And if such a refusal involves suffering financial loss, it is suffering for Christ and His truth, and will be rewarded in the day of Christ. In many cases, however, the Lord has overruled in such a situation, and things have worked out well for the person who took a stand for Christ. We must be ready for either alternative if we are to glorify God in our lives.

58. Is it wrong for a Christian to go into debt?

God's standard for Christians in business relationships is stated in Romans 12:17: "Provide things honest in the sight of all men." Vincent, in his *Word Studies,* says that "in the sight of all men" connects with "provide" rather than with the adverb "honestly," since what is honorable in the sight of men is not necessarily the standard. Men might count things honorable which the Christian might count dishonorable. The thought is that the Christian is to maintain a standard of absolute honesty in his business dealings.

Romans 13:8 makes this pronouncement: "Owe no man any thing, but to love one another: for he that loveth another hath fulfilled the law." So far as I can see, this does not refer to commercial transactions but to one's personal life. We shall always be in debt in the sense of owing love to others, but we should not be in financial debt.

In our present culture, most business is done "on credit." Some have taken Romans 13:8 as a command not to purchase anything unless it is paid for in cash, including houses and cars. But some things cannot be paid for in advance. For example, one's monthly telephone service is paid for in advance, but extra calls and tolls must be billed later. Such transactions are not in view here. Nor do we believe commercial loans are included. When one applies for such a loan, "credit" is extended because the would-be borrower furnishes adequate security, often collateral of equal value with the loan. And when one purchases a home or car by paying monthly installments, he is paying interest for the use of the money borrowed, as well as securing the amount of the loan.

We believe that Romans 13:8 refers not to the ordinary transactions involved in everyday living but to a person who overextends himself and becomes indebted for more than he has assets to cover, or ability to pay. Sometimes a person will do this to an extent which limits his giving to God, or which prevents his fulfilling his Christian responsibility. God intends that we should live well within our means, and in moderation, giving liberally to Christian work. We would then also be able to help others when we learn of a genuine need.

59. We are a young couple, and are in debt. My husband is not saved, and besides working at his job, he gambles. The other day he brought home about five hundred dollars, and I paid off some of my debts, and sent some money to my church. Was this a right thing to do?

I believe gambling is wrong for a number of reasons. Money won by gambling is money which we have not earned. It is obtained at the expense of another to whom we have not rendered any comparable value. Paul wrote in I Timothy 6:9, "But they that will be rich [are determined to be rich] fall into temptation and a snare, and into many foolish and hurtful lusts which drown men in destruction and perdition." Gambling is a scheme for "getting rich quick," as men say, and I believe it is wrong.

Money obtained by methods which, according to Scripture, are dishonorable is unacceptable to God. Then money becomes what the Bible calls "filthy lucre." Such methods of obtaining money can lead to "many sorrows" in the life of the individual.

Deuteronomy 23:18 makes it clear that money obtained improperly will not be acepted by God as an offering. God is not so much in need of money that He will accept anything offered to Him. Haggai 2:8 tells us that the silver and gold belong to the Lord, and Psalm 50:10 teaches that the world and everything in it is His.

Perhaps money obtained by gambling might be given to a public charity. However, we believe that gambling is wrong.

God is concerned that our giving should be motivated by love for Him. We can demonstrate our love for Him by giving sacrificially. (See chapters 8 and 9 of II Corinthians.) The Lord Jesus, commenting on the widow's gift of two mites, compared her gift with what others had given that day by saying, "For all they did cast in of their abundance; but she of her want did cast in all that she had, even all her living" (Mark 12:44). His comment reveals that the value of what we do for God is not its size or extent but its cost to us. King David said, "Neither will I offer burnt offerings unto the Lord my God of that which doth cost me nothing" (II Sam. 24:24).

60. What redress does a person have who has been slandered, especially when the lie has been believed by others?

We know of no promises in Scripture of immunity from false accusations, nor of redress with regard to them. Psalm 37 seems to deal with the subject, but it speaks of the solution as resting in the cutting off of evildoers. This reminds one of Asaph's resolution of his distress at the prosperity of the wicked. When he "went into the sanctuary of God" (Ps. 73:17), he understood their end. He was also reminded of his own end, and said, in verse 24, "Thou shalt guide me with thy counsel, and afterward receive me to glory."

Psalm 37:6 expresses a similar thought: "And he shall bring forth thy righteousness as the light, and thy judgment as the noon day." It is not always the case that Christians (or others) who are misrepresented are vindicated in this life, but we shall surely be vindicated before God. Perhaps this is one of the ways in which our faith is tested: Are we more concerned about *being* right, or being *acknowledged* to be right?

However, in experience we usually find that people are judged with reasonable fairness, and if we are indicted unjustly on some counts, we may well find that we are given undeserved praise on others. And God has guaranteed, in the overall experience of life, that "all things work together for good to them that love God, to them that are the called according to his purpose" (Rom. 8:28). An example of this is seen in the life of Joseph. He was slandered by Potiphar's wife, and then imprisoned in what was probably the "death row" of the prison of Pharaoh. Yet in God's time, he was released and later exalted to a place next to Pharaoh in the kingdom.

But things do not always end thus happily. Mephibosheth was slandered by his servant Ziba, and king David believed the lie (II Samuel 16). Later Mephibosheth was able to defend himself, and David, with poor grace, offered to restore half the lands he had taken from him unjustifiably. But Mephibosheth proved his right attitude about how he had been treated when he said of Ziba, "Let him take all, forasmuch as my lord the king is come again in peace unto his own house" (II Sam. 19:30). If we seek only the Lord's honor, we can bear with what is done to us, realizing that God's grace has already given us far more than we deserve.

61. Why do many Christians consider membership in secret societies wrong?

One serious objection is found in II Corinthians 6:14: "Be ye not unequally yoked together with unbelievers." Following this command is a series of questions which show the incompatibility of such a union. Secret societies include both Christians and non-Christians, yet the members of a secret society are bound together by oaths and obligations, and sometimes the nature of these is unbecoming a person who is indwelt by the Spirit of God.

Another factor to be considered is that secret societies often conduct religious exercises which are often performed by persons who do not know the Lord in a vital way; and this makes a mockery of our faith in Christ and the Bible. Sometimes a secret organization actually professes to be a kind of religion, and their members, at death, are declared to have been received into "the grand lodge on high" (provided their dues are paid up to death) regardless of faith in the Lord Jesus Christ, or lack of it.

The above are some of the basic reasons for refraining from membership in such societies. But there are other reasons. Often the social occasions held for members are something less than

spiritually edifying, while in some cases such occasions are positively defiling and disgusting. Lodge membership is a worldly
association, and hardly conforms to the Christian concept of our
obligation to glorify God in all that we do. Usually any benefits
accruing from lodge membership can be obtained in other ways.
If not, we can afford to be without them.

62. **Does Galatians 4:10-11 forbid observing birthdays or other
    anniversaries? Does not Romans 14:5 allow us to do as we
    please in such matters?**

I believe that observing birthdays or other anniversaries is op-
tional, but not on the basis of the two scriptures mentioned,
neither of which relate to this subject. These two scriptures had
to do with the continued observance of Jewish holy days by those
who had embraced Christianity. Some, because of their back-
ground teaching and experience, still felt obligated to observe
such holy days. Others, realizing that in Christianity they had to
do with spiritual realities and not the symbols of them which
Judaism afforded, did not observe such days. This applied particularly to the observance of the sabbath.

Where such observance was a matter of the individual's conscience and degree of enlightenment, as referred to in Romans
14, the Apostle Paul instructed them to bear with one another,
respecting the conscience of each other (v. 6). But where individuals seemed to attach merit to observing the requirement of
the law, and to some degree rested on such observance, the
apostle strongly condemned the system as being contrary to the
grace that is found in Christ, by faith in Him.

With regard to the observance of birthdays, Scripture says
nothing at all about it with the exception of mentioning two oc-
casions when birthdays were celebrated. One was that of Pharaoh
(Genesis 40), the other that of Herod (Matthew 14; Mark 6).
Each of these celebrations was accompanied by an execution.
Believers are not even told to celebrate the birth of Christ. In-
stead, they are to partake of the Lord's Supper as the memorial of
His atoning death. Yet I do not see any biblical ground for con-

demning those who do celebrate birthdays, provided it is done in a way which does not dishonor the Lord.

63. Why do Christians take a stand against wine when Jesus provided it at the wedding in Cana? Also, did not Paul instruct Timothy to take a little wine for his stomach's sake?

First, with regard to the marriage at Cana, we should be clear on this point: This was not, as many assume, a drunken party. The language does not support that assumption, and we believe it is derogatory to the Son of God to assume that He would aid in something that is condemned throughout Scripture. The wedding feast was orderly, and carried on in an honorable way.

We should also be clear that the Lord was not establishing the drinking of wine as a custom. It was already the custom, and the wine that was commonly drunk was of low alcoholic content, and more suitable than much of the drinking water that was available in those days, when little was known of hygiene or sanitation. In some countries it was found that drinking *tea* did not produce sickness, but drinking *water* did. They did not know that the boiling of the water to make the tea was the reason for the tea being harmless to health. In other countries, wine served the same purpose, and this was the reason for Paul's advice to Timothy (I Tim. 5:23). Another point to notice is that the Lord did not make what we call "strong drink," nor did Paul recommend Timothy's drinking anything like this.

We are living in a totally different age, and our circumstances are not at all similar to theirs. We have an abundance of good water in addition to many beverages of nonalcoholic nature. There is no necessity to resort to alcoholic beverages because of a contaminated water supply. Instead, there are numerous reasons why we should *not* indulge in alcoholic beverages. Every drunkard began with a first drink, and while some persons can drink alcohol without coming under its power, others cannot; and we do not know in advance to which group we belong. The safest thing for us is not to partake of it at all.

Besides, the sale of alcoholic beverages has become highly commercialized, and many persons are induced, by seductive advertising, to drink for questionable pleasure, and without any underlying necessity to do so. Statistics show that drinking has led to uncountable crimes and accidents, causing injury, loss, and sometimes death, to innocent people. Men have squandered money on liquor to the neglect of their homes and families. The evil effects of liquor should be a warning to us.

Wine, in the Bible, was a symbol of joy, when it was rightly used. But we must not overlook the fact that it is also used as a symbol of the judgment of God (Rev. 14:10).

I believe that in our present economy and culture the use of liquor is wrong. However, when I say this, I do not mean to imply I condemn the right use of wine by the Lord Jesus. Christ's use of wine does not justify us in using alcoholic beverages in entirely different circumstances.

64. Is it negative and therefore unscriptural to teach that Christians should abstain from alcohol, tobacco, and so on?

To discourage or forbid these things is negative, no doubt, but to say that certain teachings are unscriptural because they are negative is another matter. When the Bible says, "Thou shalt have no other gods before me," that is negative, but it is scriptural. It is a command of God, negatively expressed. Likewise, "Thou shalt not make unto thee any graven image, or any likeness of anything that is in heaven above, or that is in the earth beneath, or that is in the water under the earth: thou shalt not bow down thyself to them, nor serve them." As we go down the list of commandments, we find many of them are negatively expressed; but they are the positive commands of God.

The use of alcoholic beverages was common in ancient times, perhaps because of an inadequate water supply, and what was available was often contaminated. People did not understand the cause, but found the use of fermented beverages safer. Even in those days any abuse of the use of such beverages was condemned, and drunkenness was always a sin. In our days, when so many nonalcoholic beverages are obtainable, and when a safe and abundant water supply is usually available, and people understand what causes contamination and know how to overcome it, there is no good reason for the use of alcoholic beverages.

The seductive advertising by manufacturers of alcoholic beverages leads many young people to indulge in drinking such products, often to their eventual ruin. And when one sees but a few of the wrecks of humanity caused by the use of alcohol, not to speak of injuries, and lives lost, and damage to property caused by highway accidents in which drunken drivers are involved, one would surely wish to keep entirely clear of the use of alcoholic beverages.

The use of *tobacco* is, at best, a wasteful habit, sending one's money up in smoke, and it is increasingly being proved a menace to health.

Social dancing has in many cases helped to break down barriers of rectitude which has led to license being taken in other ways.

While Scripture also gives positive instructions for Christian living, I do not consider it unscriptural to point out these dangers to Christians. We are told (in I Cor. 6:20), "Glorify God in your body, and in your spirit, which are God's." Also (in I Cor. 10:31), "Whether therefore ye eat, or drink, or whatsoever ye do, do all to the glory of God."

65. Does Matthew 5:42 ("Give to him that asketh thee, and from him that would borrow of thee turn not thou away") mean that we must give to every beggar we meet?

No, we believe it does not. God does not encourage irresponsibility. In Ephesians 4:28 the person who formerly stole was told to steal no more but to work that he might be able "to give to him that needeth." And Paul told the Thessalonians "that if any would not work, neither should he eat." These instructions are rooted in the Old Testament law, where the Israelites were told to be always mindful of the poor among them and to help them. In cases of need, the Israelites were expected to lend money without interest ("usury" in our King James text), as we read in Exodus 22:25. But laziness and irresponsibility were never encouraged. The Israelites lived under an agrarian economy, and life was very simple for the most part. In times of sickness or other adversity, a person might require the help of his neighbors. Such help was to be given without grudging, whether by sharing physical work that had to be done, or extending financial help. "Interest" was never to be charged on loans of money, and loans were to be made even when there was no hope of their being repaid. The Lord Jesus said, in Luke 6:35, "Lend, hoping for nothing again." Probably the basic thought is, not expecting "interest" or financial gain, but the command would include willingness to consider the loan a gift in a case of special need. When the Lord said, "Your reward shall be great," He implied that it would be from God, in the day of Christ.

66. How can a Christian overcome an aversion to certain fellow believers?

The answer to this question lies in the fact that we *can* control our thoughts and attitudes. The Bible tells us to "put off" wrong thoughts and attitudes, and to "put on" other attitudes. For example, in Colossians 3:8 we are told, "Put off all these: anger, wrath, malice, blasphemy, filthy communication out of your mouth." Also, "Put on therefore, . . . bowels of mercies, kindness, humbleness of mind, meekness, longsuffering; forbearing one another, and forgiving one another, if any have a quarrel against any: even as Christ forgave you, so also do ye" (vv. 12-13).

A certain man who had lived an immoral life was truly converted to Christ. Later, when evil thoughts came to his mind, he would repeat audibly, "Dead to sin and alive to God through Jesus Christ our Lord." By an act of will he overcame his evil habits, through the power of the Holy Spirit and through use of God's Word. Any Christian can deal in the same way with anger, pride, or whatever may be the occasion of his aversion toward another. As a Christian reminds himself of the love of Christ to him, he can, in humility, put off wrong thoughts and put on those which honor the Lord.

I am not speaking of an outward show, which would only add hypocrisy to other sins but of an act of will in which the Christian refuses to entertain wrong thoughts and allows the Holy Spirit to fill his mind with right thoughts, both toward Christ and toward fellow believers. Thus Christians are enabled to love one another in their mutual faith in Christ.

67. Does a Christian violate Scripture when he wills his body for scientific use after death?

I do not know of any scripture which gives direct instruction as to the disposal of our dead bodies, though by example it suggests burial, which seems to have a spiritual import in view of the doctrine of the resurrection of the dead. As with cremation, a great deal depends on the state of soul which leads us to do it, though if a person plans to do this, he should be careful to let his family and friends know about it, else it might be a great shock to them.

Sometimes certain parts of one's body can be given for the purpose of being transplanted to another person's body. For instance, the giving of one's eyes may result in giving sight to another human being. Or if there is reason to believe that one's body could serve some useful scientific purpose which would benefit others, it would seem commendable to permit this.

Scripture emphasizes the fact that the body is part of the person and that in the resurrection—whether of saved or unsaved persons—spirit, soul, and body will be reunited for eternity. However we dispose of the body, it eventually goes into decay, so divine power must operate to raise it to life. It is wrong to desecrate the body of any human being. Whether scientific use of the body after death is considered to be desecration is a matter of individual conviction, and I know of no Scripture which would be violated by it.

68. Is professional fund-raising for Christian work in keeping with the teaching of the Bible?

While Israel was under a law of tithing to support the Tabernacle and Temple worship, and the Levites and priests who carried on the rituals, we find no specific instruction concerning giving in the church, though we do find guidelines. I Corinthians 9 and other passages clearly teach that the work of the Lord, and those who carry it on, are to be supported by God's people. The figures of speech used indicate that varied aspects of Christian work are to be supported, including church work and gospel and missionary activity. Many aspects of Christian work require the financial support of Christians.

Also, giving on the part of the children of God is taught in many scriptures. For instance, Proverbs 3:9 says: "Honor the Lord with thy substance, and with the firstfruits of all thine increase." This verse shows that giving of our means is part of our service for the Lord. Also the words, "the *firstfruits* of all thine increase," indicate that God's portion should be set aside by us before meeting any other claims.

We find also in the Bible the suggestion of proportionate giving, which is confirmed in I Corinthians 16:2: "Upon the first day of the week let every one of you lay by him in store, *as God hath prospered him.*" And in II Corinthians 9:6 we read: "He which soweth sparingly shall reap also sparingly; and he which soweth bountifully shall reap also bountifully. Every man, according as he purposeth in his heart, so let him give; not grudgingly, or of necessity: for God loveth a cheerful giver."

These scriptures all suggest voluntary giving, without pressure from others, though there is no specific instruction as to how the Christian is to use the money he gives to the Lord. Besides one's own church, he may wish to give to Christian radio programs and other spiritual services and ministries which benefit many, and to various missionary societies, some of which are undenominational or perhaps interdenominational in scope. They draw workers from various groups of Christians, and carry on an effective soul-winning work in various countries. Other works worthy of the support of Christians are Bible-training institutes, whose graduates are serving the Lord in various capacities at home and abroad.

These are just a few suggestions. Some organizations make no appeals for funds except to God in prayer. Others pray to God, but inform God's children of what is being done and what the needs are, so they can join them in prayer, and also support the work as the Lord may direct them. Other organizations make vigorous appeals, sometimes psychologically oriented to appeal to the sympathy of Christians in order to secure a larger share of Christian giving than their work might otherwise merit.

If Christian giving is to be a spiritual exercise, it cannot be governed by human sympathy. We must be much in prayer to obtain the guidance of God, so that our giving serves His will. One's own church should be supported, and also activities through which we receive help and blessing, or in which we wish to participate to bring spiritual help and blessing to others. Let us keep in mind that all our work, including our giving, will come into review in the day of Christ (I Cor. 4:1-5) for the Lord's appraisal. Professional fund raising can take Christian giving out of the sphere of spiritual concern, and insofar as it does so, it is without biblical basis.

69. Is it not contrary to Scripture for a Christian to go to war or to bear arms? Does not this violate the commands "Thou shalt not kill" and "Love thy neighbor"?

People often list proof texts to show it is wrong to kill, yet Moses, through whom the law was given, engaged in warfare. In Deuteronomy 20:16 Joshua was told, "But of the cities of these people, which the LORD thy God doth give thee for an inheritance, thou shalt save alive nothing that breatheth." Yet Joshua was under the law of Moses. The commandment, "Thou shalt not kill," has to do with murder, and does not apply to warfare.

In II Samuel 12:9 David is said to have "killed Uriah the Hittite with the sword" because David was personally involved. Of no others who died in that war was it said David that killed him. In Numbers 15:31-36 we read that God told Moses to have a man stoned to death for gathering sticks on the sabbath day. In the administration of law, capital punishment is sometimes indicated; and warfare is looked at as the administration of law on an international scale.

We can be thankful that our government permits special assignments to those who are conscientious objectors, but in my understanding of the Bible, I do not see that killing a person in warfare is ever classified as murder. The command to love one another has to do with our personal relationships and is not the basis for the administration of law, either locally or internationally.

CHRISTIAN LIVING

70. How should a "family altar" be conducted?

Before discussing the "how," I might say that the Bible has a great deal to say about godliness in the home and about bringing up one's family in the knowledge of God and His Word. In Deuteronomy 6:7 we read how the Israelite father was instructed to teach God's statutes diligently to his children, and in Ephesians 6:4 the Apostle Paul told Christians to bring up their children "in the nurture and admonition of the Lord." Such instructions to parents make mandatory some form of family Bible reading and prayer in the Christian home. I Timothy 4:5 says our food is "sanctified by the word of God and prayer," and we can be sure that this applies to all the experiences of life. This text also suggests some of the elements which constitute a family altar and perhaps also a good time to have it.

The main elements of a family altar are "the word of God" and "prayer." Many parents have found that a suitable time to have Bible reading and prayer as a family is at mealtime. In some cases meals are at irregular hours, and the family is not all together at any one meal. In such cases it would be well to plan a time for the family to be together, at whatever time of day is most suitable to the circumstances. Some families, where all are present at all meals, have the reading of Scripture and prayer after each meal. This should not be left to chance, but should be the result of prayerful planning, and consultation with all concerned.

The planning of family worship raises the question of what to read, and how large a portion. Sometimes, where there is only a man and wife, they may read several chapters. More often, especially where there are children, the reading of a single chapter will suffice, and many find it desirable to read less than a chapter. The Scripture Union issues booklets of daily readings, consisting usually of about a dozen verses, with brief comments on the passage. Others follow the Scripture passages suggested on certain calendars. Some prefer to read the Bible through consecutively.

Usually there is a "grace" or giving of thanks at the beginning of a meal, and then the reading of Scripture at the close, followed by prayer. In some families the father leads in this, while in others father and mother alternate. When children become a little older, they may be asked to read the selected Bible passage or to lead in prayer.

These are some of the methods which have been found helpful.

71. How can a family altar be carried on effectively when the children are several years apart in age?

One thing for parents to guard against is overanxiety, which may cause them to press their children beyond their physical and mental capabilities. I do not mean that parents must tailor family devotions to the age of the youngest child, but they must make allowances for the younger children, recognizing that they cannot fully enter into the more advanced reading, and providing so far as possible, something they *can* enter into. Asking them to recite a simple verse they have memorized or asking them a question they can answer will go a long way toward making them feel they are having part in the family's devotions.

Since all the children of the woman who asked this question were young, she read to them Bible stories, that is, the stories found in the Bible but presented in simpler language. It often helps when parents discuss the persons and events, expanding the child's comprehension of the meaning and relevancy of the story read to him. Often we must wait for later developments to see how effective our presentation has been, but we can be sure that continued exposure to the Word of God, and prayer, will produce an impact on the minds of the children. While I do not consider Proverbs 22:6 to be an absolute promise, it is a general principle that if we "train up a child in the way he should go. . . . when he is old, he will not depart from it."

It is also helpful to have the children memorize verses. Sometimes such memorization is done in connection with Sunday school lessons. And some parents may want their children to learn other verses besides those learned in Sunday school. The storing of God's Word in the mind is one of the greatest blessings in the life of anyone. In some families each recites a verse, whether the same one or a different verse for each one. This helps younger ones to feel they are participating equally with older ones.

72. What is the distinction between God's directive will and His permissive will? How can I know which is operating in my life in any given circumstance?

The distinction is that in the case of God's directive will He guides us by His Word and Spirit; while in the case of God's permissive will, He permits us to do what we do, even though it is not directly what He desires us to do. In any given circumstance we should seek God's guidance and honestly endeavor to do what we believe is His will for us.

A biblical promise which applies here is found in Proverbs 3:5-6: "Trust in the LORD with all thine heart; and lean not unto thine own understanding. In all thy ways acknowledge him, and he shall direct thy paths." The word *direct* means to "make straight [or, plain]." The Bible contains other similar promises, such as Matthew 6:22: "If . . . thine eye be single, thy whole body shall be full of light."

I take these Scriptures to mean that if we seek guidance from God, disregarding our own wishes or desires, He will lead us to the right thing to do. If later we wonder if we have made a mistake, we can be sure God will see us through. But if we have been governed by self-will or selfish desire, then, though God may permit what we have chosen, we cannot say He directed it.

73. How can a believer overcome worry?

Worry can be classified as a sin, because it is disobedience to such Bible commands as "Fret not" (Ps. 37:1, 7-8) and "Be anxious for nothing" (Phil. 4:6, marginal reading).

The habit of worry, once formed, becomes difficult to break. Someone has said that "worry is the interest which people pay on borrowed trouble." A brief answer, then, to this question would be, "Don't borrow trouble." This is not a mere cliché but part of basic Christianity. We profess to trust Christ for our eternal welfare; can we not trust Him for the comparatively minor necessities of life?

It is a principle of Scripture that we exhibit our inward state by outward acts and words. "Out of the abundance of the heart the mouth speaketh" (Matt. 12:34). We demonstrate that we love God by loving our brothers in Christ (I John 4:20). By using the same reasoning, we might say that worry demonstrates that our profession of confidence in God is not genuine.

In Matthew 6:25-34 we read direct commands by the Lord Jesus not to worry. The entire passage teaches us that we are to trust God for food, clothing, shelter, and for the exigencies of life in general. Elsewhere in Scripture we are exhorted to take responsibility to make proper provision for our needs, but we should beware of developing the harmful (and sinful) habit of worrying about such things. God has promised to care for us.

Philippians 4:6-7 gives the cure for worry: "Be careful [anxious] for nothing; but in every thing by prayer and supplication with thanksgiving let your requests be made known unto God. And the peace of God, which passeth all understanding, shall keep your hearts and minds through Christ Jesus." If we are convinced the subject of our concern is something legitimate and proper for us, we can bring it to God with earnest supplication to undertake for us in the matter. Then we must leave the matter in His hands, and rest in the assurance that in His wisdom, He will either give what we ask or give us something better. Faith enables us to share God's own peace about the matter, and we do not worry. Worry is lack of confidence in God.

74. How can we discover the talents that God has given to us for His service?

Scripture gives no specific instruction concerning this. We are told in Ephesians 4 that spiritual gifts are given by our ascended Lord, and the word used is that used for a "present." In I Corinthians 12, spiritual gifts are referred to as charismatic gifts, manifestations of the Holy Spirit. In each of these Scripture passages, some of the gifts in view are listed, and in I Corinthians 12 to 14 we find instructions about how these gifts are to be used. But I know of no passage which teaches how we are to discern what gifts we may have.

In the Book of Proverbs there are several references to "gifts," which some consider to refer to bribes which one might offer a judge, and so gain his favor. However, these may be taken to refer to spiritual gifts. If we take them as such, we get some insight as to how gifts become known. Proverbs 17:8 says, "A gift is as a precious stone in the eyes of him that hath it: whithersoever it turneth, it prospereth." This seems to say that as a person goes about serving the Lord in whatever way is open to him, he discovers (and of course others do also) that he has a God-given ability along certain lines. "It prospers."

In Proverbs 18:16 we read, "A man's gift maketh room for him, and bringeth him before great men." This is to say, as a person cultivates and seeks to develop his gift, it becomes apparent to all. The proper use of his gift will bring him into the place God has designed for him. He will not need to resort to various maneuvers to obtain opportunity for the full use of the gift God has given. He who gave the gift will provide the desirable scope for its use.

Proverbs 25:14 warns, "Whoso boasteth himself of a false gift is like clouds and wind without rain." This supposes a person through natural cleverness seeking acceptance as one having a spiritual gift from God. He may have all the outward display suggested by "clouds and wind," but the desired blessing does not follow. His efforts are "without rain," which Isaiah 55:10 identifies as the means God uses to bring forth increase.

75. What does the Bible teach about labor-management relationships?

The Word of God views all the problems of life as being rooted in what we *are*. What we *do* expresses our inward state. If the inward state is right, it produces right actions, and vice versa. Consequently, Scripture speaks to both masters and servants with regard to their obligations to both God and man, rather than trying to correct current social evils, which included slavery. In the Bible we find a denunciation by the Lord Jesus of oppression by the rich and a prophecy by James about a time when the tables would be reversed, and the rich would become the oppressed.

The Lord Jesus denounced those who "devoured widows' houses," as well as those who laid heavy burdens on others but would not lift a finger to share the burden (Matt. 23:14, 4). Other social ills were also mentioned, though it was chiefly to remind the Jews that they were the professed people of God and owed it to Him rightly to represent His character.

In Paul's letter to the Colossians he wrote: "Servants, obey in all things your masters according to the flesh; not with eyeservice as menpleasers; but in singleness of heart, fearing God: and whatsoever ye do, do it heartily, as to the Lord, and not unto men; knowing that of the Lord ye shall receive the reward of the inheritance: for ye serve the Lord Christ" (3:22-24). The word *servants* is actually the Greek word for "slaves," and yet Paul asserts that their service was acknowledged by the Lord as being rendered to Him. This dignifies the labor of a Christian, and gives it divine significance and value, even where it is rendered on the basis of human bondage.

Paul had a word also for masters: "Give unto your servants that which is just and equal, knowing that ye also have a Master in heaven" (Col. 4:1). Masters, too, must render an account of their lives to the Lord, and so should always deal in fairness with those who serve them. In both cases Paul stressed the fact that the ultimate values of life are found in Christ's presence, rather than on earth.

James, in chapter 5 of his letter, said: "Go to now, ye rich men, weep and howl for the miseries that shall come upon you. Your riches are corrupted, and your garments are motheaten. . . . Behold, the hire of the laborers who have reaped down your fields, which is of you kept back by fraud, crieth: and the cries of them which have reaped are entered into the ears of the Lord of sabaoth [or, of hosts]."

From this passage we learn that James foresaw a time when working men would rise up against those who had exploited them, and "heap miseries" upon the rich. We have seen something of this in the strikes not uncommon in our day, which cause distress not only to the rich, in the interruption of their business, but also to the public who may not be directly involved in the dispute. James offered no cure, but encouraged those he called "brethren" (fellow believers) to be patient until the coming of the Lord, when all shall be made right.

76. Should I witness for Christ to everyone I meet?

Often a person who determines to speak to everyone he meets ends up by speaking to no one. If we aim to speak to *one* person, we are far more likely to speak not only to one but to several, one after another. But when we speak of "witnessing," this requires definition, for witnessing includes not only what we say but the way we act. In Acts 4:13 we read: "Now when they saw the boldness of Peter and John, and perceived that they were unlearned and ignorant men, they marvelled; and they took knowledge of them, that they had been with Jesus." There was something about these men which made an impact on others—an impact far greater than might have been expected of them. Their opponents recognized that this grew out of their having "been with Jesus."

This kind of witness is hard to refute. The Apostle Peter said, "For so is the will of God, that with well doing ye may put to silence the ignorance of foolish men" (I Pet. 2:15). Peter was telling those believers that even though men were not at that time impressed (they spoke against them as evil doers), "They may, by your good works which they shall behold, glorify God in the day of visitation" (v. 12). In this respect a believer is a witness wherever he goes. An example is seen in the life of Jacob's son Joseph, who, in spite of a succession of events adverse to him, won the confidence of his successive masters by his reliability. Whether in humiliation or exaltation, he "adorned" the doctrine which he professed by his winsome manner of life.

However, it is desirable also to witness by word. The witness of life alone may be misunderstood unless some explanation is given. Sometimes this can be done in conversation, but a great many persons who are not convincing conversationalists find that giving out tracts is a fruitful form of witnessing for Christ. If a person wants to do some seed-sowing every day, it would be well for him to give a tract to someone in the early part of the day, if possible. Ecclesiastes 11:6 says: "In the morning sow thy seed, and in the evening withhold not thy hand: for thou knowest not whether [which] shall prosper, . . . or whether they both shall be alike good." And Isaiah 32:20 says: "Blessed are ye that sow beside all waters." From these texts we gather that we can witness any time, and should do so everywhere. In Psalm 126:6 we find an important additional feature: "He that goeth forth and *weepeth,* bearing precious seed, shall doubtless come again with rejoicing, bringing his sheaves with him."

Therefore, to be witnesses for Christ we need to be constantly aware that we are in this world for Him, and show by our manner of life that He has met the needs of our life. We also need to be available for the Holy Spirit to use to speak a word in season as He gives opportunity. We may hinder His working if we try to "buttonhole" everyone we meet. We must remember that it is the Holy Spirit who brings conviction to men; our part is to witness.

77. Should Christians continue witnessing to relatives who show resentment because of such a witness?

The questioner tells of a grown son who admits smoking and drinking when out with others, and who says, "Quit preaching to me." The questioner also asks whether Christians should not rather witness to those with a more open mind. But while witnessing to those who more readily receive our testimony may be more gratifying, I believe we are responsible to continue witnessing to those among whom God has placed us, and especially to those with whom we have a close relationship.

However, witnessing includes more than speaking to people about the Lord, or putting tracts and literature into the hands of the persons to whom we are witnessing. The Apostle Peter, in I Peter 3, gave instruction to the woman who has a husband who is not a believer to be subject to him (not, of course, in anything that would be positively dishonoring to God) in order that she may "without a word" (as it is literally) win him by her behavior (as the word "conversation" should be translated).

This suggests that we win people who are not receptive to the spoken or printed word by showing the love of God and the humility of patience. It is easier to preach than it is to practice Christian virtues. However, consistent Christian living often opens people's hearts where preaching does not. Once their hearts are open, *then* it is the Word of God which gives them the knowledge of God and His salvation. We cannot force the gospel upon unwilling ears.

Scripture says, "He that winneth souls is wise" (Prov. 11:30). A patient, godly life has tremendous winning power.

78. How does a weight, mentioned in Hebrews 12:1, differ from sin?

The verse says: "Let us lay aside every weight, and the sin which doth so easily beset us, and let us run with patience the race that is set before us."

Some things which are not inherently sinful may become hindrances to us as we run the race of life. Many persons give most of their spare time to things which, though not wrong, are not purposeful. Such things are a weight in the sense that these persons lose the spiritual gain they might have had if they had used their time more profitably.

Some Christians put thousands of dollars into hobbies which are interesting, and certainly not sinful. Yet in the day of Christ, when they give account of the stewardship God has given them, they may find this money could have been invested for the furtherance of the Lord's work, and so have borne fruit for their own reward "in that day." I am not attempting to judge others. Each of us is accountable to God. But I am suggesting areas of life about which Christians need to be concerned lest they allow something not wrong in itself to become a hindrance to their fruitfulness to God. All of life is a stewardship, and in the presence of God we shall not be credited with what we possessed, but with what we wisely used, in His name, for the furtherance of His interests and for the well-being of those around us.

79. Why do Christians fail?

This question requires more than a single simple answer, because there are many causes for failure, either singly, or in combination. In II Peter 1:5-11 we are told of seven things we should "add" to our faith. Some translate: "have in your faith." Just as a flower unfolds, and added features are seen as it does so, so the Christian's faith is to come to full bloom and have in it these seven things: virtue, knowledge, temperance, patience, godliness, brotherly love [margin], charity [or, love].

We are told that "if these things be in you, and abound, they make you that ye shall neither be barren [idle] nor unfruitful in the knowledge of our Lord Jesus Christ." This is the immediate benefit; but verse 10 adds, "For if ye do these things, ye shall never fall." Hence the cure for Christian failure is to "give diligence" to develop in our faith the features of Christian character described in the list given.

The word "virtue" originally meant courage, or excellence. It probably implies standing boldly for Christ. If we do so, we shall soon find we need "knowledge" of God's Word, both to support the stand we take and to win others to it. "Temperance" is self-control, so that living is not mere self-expression; rather, we allow the Spirit of God to work in and through us. "Patience" involves bearing the trials of life in the strength of God, so that we are triumphant in them. "Godliness" implies piety of life; in the Christian it means Godlikeness, though that is not the strict meaning of the word itself.

"Brotherly kindness" is simply "love of the brethren." It implies not only outward association in church fellowship but inward unity of heart and mind in the recognition that we possess a common life and have a common Saviour and destiny, and are fighting in a common cause. "Charity" is old English for "love," and implies our love for God in response to His love for us. This will deepen our love for the brethren and give us an attitude of love toward all others. "Giving diligence" is from a word which involves making haste, so we have the thought of making it our prompt and vigorous concern to develop our Christian life and character. Unless we do, we are likely to fall.

80. If the believer is not to come into judgment for his sins because of the atonement of Christ, does this mean that the believer's sins do not affect rewards at the judgment seat of Christ?

When Scripture speaks of the believer not coming into judgment for his sins it is referring to his having to pay the penalty of them. This was why the Lord Jesus Christ died as He did. Jehovah laid on Him the iniquity of us all, and for those who believe in Him, this judgment is already past. But sin does grieve the Holy Spirit and quenches His working in us. Sin also breaks our communion with God as our Father. Also we often have to bear the physical and earthly results of our sins; so sin is a serious matter.

In evaluating our lives at the judgment seat of Christ, we are to remember what Paul said in I Corinthians 4:5, "Therefore judge nothing before the time, until the Lord come, who both will bring to light the hidden things of darkness, and will make manifest the counsels of the hearts: and then shall every man have [his] praise of God." The mention of "the hidden things of darkness" shows clearly that these are considered in connection with the giving of rewards. Sin mars our usefulness now in true spiritual power, and will be manifested to our loss in that day.

CONTRADICTIONS

81. Does the Bible contradict itself?

We believe the Bible does not contradict itself, though making such a statement is not satisfactory, since it is open to challenge with every difficulty anyone can bring up. However, we can make some comments on this subject which may be helpful.

Usually persons who make the claim that "the Bible is full of contradictions" have not read the Bible itself. They have read what someone else has written about apparent contradictions in the Bible, and have only a vague notion of what is involved. Rarely do they know any actual variations in the text of Scripture which might support such claims.

Many supposed contradictions are due to faulty text. It must be remembered that for centuries all copies of the Bible were made by hand. Anyone familiar with the difficulties involved will marvel that there are not many more inaccuracies in some copies of the text. But apart from the few inaccuracies that appear, most of the supposed difficulties are the result of not reading the Bible carefully. It was carefully written, by divine inspiration, and both its insertions and omissions are designed. Often a person who fails to notice fine distinctions comes to the false conclusion that there are contradictions in the Bible.

Also, the Bible is understood by each generation in the light of the general knowledge available to that generation. People often confuse expositions of the Bible, given at various times, with what the Bible itself says. The Bible cannot be held responsible for what men have drawn from it, even with good intention. The question is whether the text itself is committed to a wrong proposition.

Actually, it is amazing that a book of such antiquity is so completely free from the absurdities of the time in which it was written, especially since its writing covered a period of some fifteen hundred years. It is reassuring to know that hundreds of alleged inaccuracies and apparent contradictions have been examined and satisfactorily explained. This gives us confidence that if people knew and understood all the facts, they would find neither inaccuracy nor contradiction in the Bible.

82. **How can we reconcile the statements in Exodus 24:10 ("And they saw the God of Israel") and John 1:18 ("No man hath seen God at any time")?**

Some think that Moses and those who accompanied him (Exodus 24:9) saw a visible manifestation of God's glory and that the statement in Deuteronomy 4:12 refers to this, since verses 10 and 11 speak of their being gathered under the mountain to hear the voice of God. "And the LORD spake unto you out of the midst of the fire: ye heard the voice of the words, but saw no similitude; only ye heard a voice." In this view the mention of "feet" in Exodus 24:10 is taken as figurative, meaning simply that they saw what resembled a pavement under the manifestation of God's glory.

Others believe that we are to take the feet literally, and these assume that the Lord appeared in human form on this occasion, as He did on other occasions recorded in the Old Testament. (For instance, the man who wrestled with Jacob was none other than the Lord in human form.) That view would not conflict with John 1:18, since it would have been the Son of God, and not the Father, who appeared in this way.

83. **How can we reconcile II Kings 8:26 and II Chronicles 22:2? One says Ahaziah was 22 years old, the other 42.**

Ellicott's Commentary says, with reference to the passage in II Chronicles: "An error of transcription. II Kings 8:26, *twenty and two;* and so the Syriac and Arabic: the LXX has 'twenty.' Ahaziah could not have been forty when he succeeded [to the throne], because his father was only forty when he died (ch. 21:20)."

In those days sons of the royal families in the East often had wives and concubines at an early age, so there is no problem on that score, but reporting the age of Ahaziah as 42 seems clearly an error in transcription. It must be remembered that in those days all copies of manuscripts had to be made by hand. Extreme care was taken to make accurate copies, but occasionally, as here, a discrepancy crept into the official text. Such errors are comparatively few, and sufficient information is available elsewhere in Scripture to correct such errors.

84. Does not I Corinthians 2:15 contradict Luke 6:37? One says we judge everything, and the other tells us to judge nothing.

I believe there is no contradiction between these two passages.

Luke 6:37 says, "Judge not, and ye shall not be judged: condemn not, and ye shall not be condemned: forgive, and ye shall be forgiven." It should be noticed, first, that the word *judge* is used in the sense of condemnation; and, second, that the word obviously refers to men's dealings with each other. God does not forgive people because of their tolerance of the faults and failures of others. God's forgiveness is received only by faith in Christ, through the merits of His atoning blood.

I Corinthians 2:14-15 reads: "The natural man receiveth not the things of the Spirit of God: for they are foolishness unto him: neither can he know them, for they are spiritually discerned. But he that is spiritual judgeth all things, yet he himself is judged of no man." Here the word translated "judgeth" and "judged" has a prefix which gives it the sense of discernment; and the word used twice in verse 15 is identical with that translated "discerned" in verse 14.

Seen in its context, these verses are not teaching that a spiritual man condemns everyone. Rather they state that a spiritual man has divinely given discernment. The natural man, on the other hand, does not understand the things of the Spirit of God, and so does not understand the actions and motives of one who is spiritual.

FUTURE EVENTS

85. What is the order of prophetic events from this time, according to your understanding of the Bible?

I understand the Bible to teach that believers living today should be looking for the coming of Christ described in I Thessalonians 4:13-18, which we refer to as the "rapture" of the Church (from the Latin term for "catching away"). I take this to be "the blessed hope" of Titus 2:13. This is the event the Thessalonian converts waited for (I Thess. 1:9-10). We read of this also in Philippians 3:20-21 and I Corinthians 15:51 and elsewhere.

Then will follow in heaven the judgment seat of Christ described in I Corinthians 3:11-15. This is referred to as "the day of Christ" in Philippians 1:10 and 2:16. At the same time there will begin on earth what is called "the day of the Lord." This is the time when the Lord will begin to deal with men in judgment. We read of this in I Thessalonians 5:1-9 and many other passages. It is "the time of Jacob's trouble" (Jer. 30:7), but will also include the Gentile nations (Joel 3:9-14) and the unbelieving and apostate elements of the professing church (Rev. 2:22). Amos 5:18-20 and Zephaniah 1:14-18 give us some idea of the character of this period, the description of which is amplified in many passages.

At the end of this period the Lord will come in person to the earth (Matt. 24:29-31) and will judge the nations (Matt. 25:31-46). This will eventuate in the setting up of Christ's millennial kingdom (Rev. 20:1-6). The characteristics of this kingdom are described in many prophecies, of which Isaiah 11 and 65 are examples. Revelation 20:7-10 shows this period will end in a great rebellion, with Satan being at that time cast into the lake of fire.

Revelation 20:11-15 shows that the final judgment of the unsaved will occur at this time, and will be followed by the introduction of the eternal state (Rev. 21:1-7). II Peter 3:9-13 foretells the purging of the present order of things to make way for the "new heavens and new earth wherein dwelleth righteousness." We understand this to be a fixed state for the coming eternity, and it is what is elsewhere called the kingdom of God, or of the Father.

We may add that we understand Revelation 21:9ff. to be a kind of recapitulation, referring back to the millennial kingdom rather than to the eternal state described in the preceding verses. This will account for "the healing of the nations" in Revelation 22:2, which would not be necessary in the eternal state, where sin and its effects are forever abolished.

86. **If at the coming of the Lord for us every believer is caught up from the earth, how could this be a secret rapture, as some teach, even though the event might not be visible to mortal eyes? Would not those who have heard this teaching be aware of what will then happen?**

This question supposes that the rapture of the Church will take place under otherwise tranquil circumstances, so that the sudden disappearance of believers in Christ could be readily identified. But I know of nothing in Scripture to suggest that this event will occur in that way. If, instead, there should be an atomic explosion, or a sudden declaration of war, with perhaps additional catastrophic events such as earthquakes, whirlwinds, or other natural phenomena which would completely distract the minds of men, it does not seem likely, in my opinion, that they would notice that believers had disappeared.

In the case of such catastrophes, unbelievers might also be destroyed, and since, of those remaining, there would undoubtedly be a considerable number of persons professing Christianity who have never experienced the new birth, no one would be able to discern that the true believers in Christ had been caught up to heaven. That it is more likely to be this way seems probable to me from the fact that Scripture says of those who previously heard the gospel and did not believe it, "For this cause God shall send them strong delusion, that they should believe a lie" (II Thess. 2:11). If they will recognize that the rapture has taken place, it would seem they would more likely believe the truth.

87. If all believers will be caught up at the rapture of the Church, how will people become converted to Christ during the period of the Great Tribulation? Who will witness to them?

In Revelation 7, which describes events which I understand will take place in the early part of the Tribulation, 144,000 are sealed for God out of the twelve tribes of Israel. We are not told the basis on which this is done, though every precedent of Scripture would indicate that God would not do this except on the ground of their having faith in Him and in His Word and promises. There may be a parallel to this in the experience of the Apostle Paul.

In I Timothy 1:15-16 Paul wrote, "This is a faithful saying, and worthy of all acceptation, that Christ Jesus came into the world to save sinners; of whom I am chief. Howbeit, for this cause I obtained mercy, that in me first Jesus Christ might show forth all longsuffering for a pattern to them which should hereafter believe on him to life everlasting." The word *chief* is elsewhere translated "first." This fits very well with the verse following, which indicates that Paul's conversion was to be a pattern to those who would later believe in Christ. And in I Corinthians 15:8 he described himself "as one born out of due time," or prematurely born.

All of this implies that Paul's conversion may be a pattern of how God will bring this remnant of Israel to Himself. God, who knows the hearts of all men, saw that while Paul was bitterly opposed to Christ, his opposition was carried on in the ignorance of unbelief (I Tim. 1:13) and that inwardly he had an honest desire to please God. This became evident when Christ revealed Himself to Paul when he was on the way to Damascus. Paul immediately believed, and gave himself unreservedly to the Lord. So, I take it, after all the believers are caught up from the earth, the Lord will reveal Himself in a direct way to this remnant of Israel, as He did to Paul, and thus provide the nucleus for a fresh testimony to Himself on the earth.

88. If believers are caught up at the rapture of the Church, and those who believe during the Tribulation are martyred, over whom will Christ reign when He comes to establish His kingdom?

It is true that many believers in Christ will be martyred during the Tribulation period, but it is not correct to say that all of them will be. In my understanding, God will miraculously preserve some, as the 144,000 mentioned in Revelation 7. Others, too, will escape the horrors of that time. This seems involved in what is said in Matthew 25:31-40, in what we usually refer to as the judgment of the "sheep" and the "goats." These sheep evidently are persons who will shelter the Lord's brethren (believing Jews), even though it will mean risking their life to do so. Their salvation will not be based on these works, but the works will be cited as the strongest proof of their faith. Revelation 7 tells of a multitude of Gentile believers, so great they could not be numbered.

Not only will these believers enter into Christ's earthly kingdom (Matt. 25:34), but it is thought by some that other inhabitants of the earth, who will be living in areas not involved in the rule of the "beast" of Revelation 13, will be given an opportunity to submit themselves to the rule of the Messiah. If they submit to this in faith, it will mean that they become saved, receiving Christ as their Saviour and King. But several passages in the Psalms suggest the possibility of a false profession. Such would enter the kingdom, but would not be saved. Psalm 18:44 has been rendered: "The strangers shall feign obedience to me."

89. **We have been taught that no one who hears the gospel now, and does not believe it, will be saved after the rapture of the Church. Would not reason indicate that some would repent and believe when they realize believers are gone and they are left behind?**

We are not left to reason in this matter. Scripture plainly states, in II Thessalonians 2:12, "That they all might be damned [or, judged] who believed not the truth, but had pleasure in unrighteousness." This verse, together with its context, indicates that when a person trifles with the grace of God, he is in danger of his day of grace running out and of being lost forever. We do not know when we shall die, and we do not know when the Lord will come and take His Church home to heaven. Either event will end the day of grace, i.e., one's opportunity to be saved. It is dangerous for anyone to neglect the salvation of his soul. The gospel message is one of urgency. "Behold, now is the accepted time; behold, now is the day of salvation" (II Cor. 6:2).

90. **What is meant by Daniel's "seventieth week"?**

The "seventy weeks of Daniel," as the prophecy is commonly called, is found in chapter 9 of the Book of Daniel, and it treats chiefly the time element in the prophetic calendar, whereas most prophecies have to do with the events only, without regard to the time. In this prophecy God revealed to Daniel that seventy "sevens" (or "weeks") were determined upon Daniel's people, who were, of course, the nation of Israel. By comparing this passage with parallel passages, we find that these "sevens" were weeks of years, and not days; and the context confirms this.

This prophecy states that beginning with an event whose date can be verified by historical records, certain events would take place, leading up to the advent of "Messiah the prince." This would occupy sixty-nine of the seventy weeks, but the prophecy shows that there would then be a hiatus, caused by the cutting off of Messiah. Our version says, "but not for himself," though the margin reads: "and shall have nothing." This indicates that the completion of what was to take place in the seventy weeks' time would be delayed.

The remaining "seventieth week" of this prophecy is described in verse 27, and the events correspond with other prophecies concerning what is called the Great Tribulation, immediately preceding the coming of Christ to establish His kingdom. In our understanding, this "Tribulation" follows the "rapture" of the Church described in I Thessalonians 4:13-18.

91. What is the meaning of "Babylon the Great" in Revelation 17? Does this term have reference to a particular religious group?

This passage has its roots in the prophecy of Daniel 7, which shows that "the times of the Gentiles" would comprise four successive world empires and that the last of these would have two forms. The second of these two forms would be in existence at the coming of the Son of man, referring to Christ's second advent.

Revelation 13 gives additional details about this fourth empire, showing its Satanic nature, and how this will express itself. Then chapter 17 gives us further identification of this empire, with additional details. This is a separate vision from chapter 16, which had carried the readers of the Book of Revelation on to the actual coming of Christ. This vision (in chapter 17) concerns itself chiefly with a harlot who rides upon a scarlet beast which has seven heads and ten horns. This description identifies this empire with the beast of chapter 13, and locates it geographically by referring to the "seven mountains on which the woman sitteth." In New Testament times the one important city known to be built on seven hills was Rome, and most Bible students make that identification here.

This beast represents the political power which will be prominent in the last part of "the times of the Gentiles." The woman who rides this beast is believed to represent the apostate elements of Christendom which will be left in the world when the true Church of Christ is caught up into heaven. A chaste virgin represents the true Church (II Cor. 11:2), while a bad woman rep-

resents the apostate church (Rev. 2:20). Chapters 17 and 18
of Revelation indicate a secularistic, apostate church. We believe
this church comprises all professed Christians who have not experienced the new birth, and is not confined to any one segment
of Christendom.

92. Does the "Tribulation" take place immediately after the rap-
ture of the Church?

If we identify the "Tribulation" period with the seventieth week
of Daniel—and to me this seems to be the correct identification—
then its beginning would be coincident with the beginning of *that*
period. While, in my understanding of the prophetical calendar,
the Tribulation is the next event after the rapture of the Church,
I do not know of anything which links them directly together.

In Daniel 9 there is a break in the continuity of the seventy-
week prophecy, after the first 69 weeks, which are continuous.
The length of the break is not revealed, and the seventieth week
begins with the signing of a covenant between a certain "prince
that shall come" and those who shall in that day represent the
nation of Israel in the land of Palestine. While this could take
place at any time after the rapture of the Church, Scripture does
not relate it to any event which may have preceded it.

It seems likely that the rapture of the Church will make catastrophic changes in the life of the nations, so there would need
to be a very quick reorganization of the Western European nations in particular. This could easily bring about conformity to
the circumstances described in prophecy. But if there is a considerable time-lapse between the rapture of the Church and the
Tribulation it would not violate any statement of Scripture.

93. During the Tribulation will the gospel message be different
from the gospel message for our day?

The basic gospel message is the same for all dispensations, and
may be stated simply in the terms given in Ephesians 2:8-9, ". . by
grace are ye saved through faith; and that not of yourselves: it is

the gift of God: not of works, lest any man should boast." Other scriptures establish the fact that God forgives sin only because of the atoning blood of Christ, and that His salvation is made effective by the regenerating power of the Holy Spirit. See I John 1:7; Hebrews 9:22; John 1:12-13; 3:1-8, and others. In Ephesians 2:8-9 the phrase "by grace" means we do not deserve salvation, and "by faith" implies one's submission to God, which involves repentance.

It may be difficult for us who have the completed Bible, and who know of the finished work of atonement, to understand how anyone can be saved without some theological knowledge of the gospel message. Yet it is evident that before Christ came many persons were saved by believing the measure of revelation which they had received. Even before the Bible began to be written there were many heroes of faith, such as Abel, Enoch, Noah, and others (Hebrews 11) whose knowledge of the theology involved in the gospel was minimal, yet whose faith in God and what He had revealed to them was great.

While salvation always centered in the promised Saviour, much of the Old Testament revelation points to His advent in glory to reign over the earth. If we take Matthew 24:14 to refer to the Tribulation period, we find that "this gospel of the kingdom shall be preached in all the world for a witness to all nations." This indicates a change of emphasis to one which points to Christ as Saviour and coming King. However, there will be no change in the basic facts of the gospel. The ground of forgiveness, and the requirements for man's reception of its benefits will remain the same.

94. Who are the beast and the false prophet of Revelation 20:10?

The "beast and the false prophet" mentioned in Revelation 20:10 are the same persons as those described in chapter 13 of that book as two beasts. The first is described as a composite of the first three beasts of Daniel 7, and this suggests that he is in some way identified with the fourth beast of Daniel 7. Since that prophecy indicates that the fourth beast will exist in the last days, at the time of the second coming of Christ, this beast of Revelation 13 seems to be the fulfillment of that.

The second beast of Revelation 13 is described as coming up out of the "earth," whereas the first came up out of the "sea." Since the sea generally represents the nations, and the "land" the nation of Israel, some have thought these two beasts represent certain rulers who will come into power in the closing days of this dispensation, or at least, in the time of tribulation which is to follow it, according to many Old Testament prophecies.

Also, since the second beast is said to have "two horns like a lamb" (Rev. 13:11), some have thought that this refers to a personal antichrist or, at any rate, to a religious leader, whereas the first will be a political leader. However, these two men will work together, the second being later designated "the false prophet." It is believed they will head up the rebellion against the authority of Christ described in Psalm 2 and many other Scriptures. Both men are said to be energized by Satan, and will have supernatural powers, according to II Thessalonians 2.

95. Please explain the terms "the terrible day of the Lord," "the Great Tribulation," and "Armageddon." How are these related?

In Joel 2:30-31 we read, "And I will show wonders in the heavens and in the earth, blood, and fire, and pillars of smoke. The sun shall be turned into darkness, and the moon into blood, before the great and terrible day of the Lord come." When Peter refers to this in Acts 2:20, our version reads "that great and notable day of the Lord."

Other Old Testament references indicate the day of the Lord will be the time when God will deal with men in judgment, after the Church is caught up to heaven as described in I Thessalonians 4:13-18. The nature of these judgments is such that this period is called, in Daniel 12:1, "a time of trouble [or, tribulation], such as never was since there was a nation even to that same time." The Lord Jesus used similar phraseology, in Matthew 24:21, in referring to this same period. See also Revelation 7:14, where "great tribulation" is literally, "the tribulation, the great one."

The term "great tribulation" does not refer to the ordinary tribulations which have always been the lot of the child of God in this sinful world (John 16:33), nor even an intensification of them. These are from the world, but the Great Tribulation is the outpouring of the wrath of God upon men on the earth. Revelation 6:15-17 tells us that "the kings of the earth, and the great men, and the rich men, and the chief captains, and the mighty men, and every bondman, and every free man, . . . said to the mountains and rocks, Fall on us, and hide us from the face of him that sitteth on the throne, and from the wrath of the Lamb: for the great day of his wrath is come; and who shall be able to stand?"

The Great Tribulation, then, and "the terrible day of the Lord" are the same period of time, and the events of that period will have the effect of gathering out of the earth the things that offend, so that Christ's kingdom can be set up in peace and righteousness, according to many scriptures. The battle of Armageddon is one feature of that period, mentioned in Revelation 16:16-21. Here there seems to be a combination of conflict among men and judgments from God out of heaven.

96. Is there a scriptural basis for the idea of a "revived Roman Empire"?

I believe so, though speculations on this subject which did not have biblical foundation have done much to discredit the study of prophecy. Periodically people have seen a similarity between conditions prevailing in their time and certain biblical passages, and have assumed that prophecy was therefore in process of fulfillment. Such persons as Napoleon, the German Kaiser Wilhelm, Adolph Hitler, and Benito Mussolini have been identified as the Antichrist. Fanciful and totally unfounded tales have been told of secret preparations for acts which would consummate what is foretold in the prophecies of the Bible. When these identifications have been proved untrue by the course of events, many people have concluded that all study of the prophetical writings is vain.

But there are facts of prophecy which cannot be ignored. The image of the man revealed to Nebuchadnezzar in a dream (Dan. 2) showed four empires, each contiguous to the other; yet the fourth continued until the second advent of Christ, though changing to a slightly different form at its extremity. Likewise God revealed to Daniel by visions (Dan. 7) that "the times of the Gentiles" would consist of four successive world empires, in this case represented by wild beasts. The fourth of these also was in existence, though in a slightly changed form, at the time of the setting up of the kingdom of the Son of man.

The first three of these world powers are identified by name in the Book of Daniel. They are Babylon, Medo-Persia, and Greece. The fourth is not named, and various identifications have been made of it. To me, the most satisfactory is that it refers to the Roman Empire, which certainly was the leading world power in the time of Christ. Only one ruler in those days would think of issuing "a decree . . . that all the world shall be taxed" (Luke 2:1).

Since the prophecies in Daniel to which we have referred show that this fourth empire will have some form of existence at the second advent of Christ, Bible students speak of a "revived Roman Empire." They do not mean necessarily the same political organization, nor that there must be of necessity the precise geographical limits of that empire. In fact, it would be difficult to know what those limits were when it existed before. But since the prophecies relating to Christ's first coming were fulfilled literally, I see no reason why those relating to His second coming should not likewise have literal fulfillment. So I believe there is a biblical basis for believing that there will be a world power at the end time which will correspond to the Roman Empire of Christ's time.

An example of possible differences between the past and future empires referred to is that the one yet to come is said to consist of a consolidation of ten kingdoms (or governments). So far as we know, this was never the case with the Roman Empire as it existed in history. Yet the iron of the fourth kingdom in Nebuchadnezzar's vision extended to the toes, and it was the fourth beast of Daniel's vision which had the ten horns at the time of the end, indicating some kind of continuity.

97. Can you explain Matthew 24:15: "When you see the abomination of desolation spoken of by Daniel the prophet stand in the holy place"? Also, has this event happened already?

There are several references in Daniel which use similar phraseology. In chapter 8 (verse 13) he speaks of "the transgression of desolation"; and in chapter 11 (verse 31) there is a reference to "the abomination that maketh desolate." Both these texts are believed to refer to an event which took place when the Syrian king Antiochus Epiphanes overran Jerusalem and defiled the Temple. This was permitted by God as a judgment on the nation of Israel because of their sins.

However, both these references are followed by a description of other events which are said to be for "the latter time of their kingdom" (8:23), or "the time of the end" (11:35). There is a related passage also in Daniel 9:27, and the statement by the Lord Jesus in Matthew 24 shows that there remains a future fulfillment of these prophecies. This double fulfillment of portions of God's Word is sometimes called "the law of double reference."

The one question is, did our Lord refer to the desecration and destruction of the Temple by the Romans in A.D. 70, as many expositors think, or did He speak of events which still lie in the future? That Christ referred to events which are still future seems clear, since He stated that at the time of the setting up of this "abomination of desolation" there would be "great tribulation, such as was not since the beginning of the world to this time, no, nor ever shall be."

Some would relate this to the destruction of Jerusalem, because of the incredible hardships and suffering endured by the Jews at that time. But in Matthew 24:29 the Lord Jesus added: "Immediately after the tribulation of those days shall the sun be darkened, and the moon shall not give her light, and the stars shall fall from heaven, and the powers of the heavens shall be shaken: and then shall appear the sign of the Son of man in heaven: . . . and they shall see the Son of man coming in the clouds of heaven with power and great glory." Consequently, we take it that what our Lord referred to in Matthew 24:15 is an event still future, and corresponds with the event described in somewhat similar language in Daniel 9:27.

98. Where in the Bible can I find mention of antichrist, and who is he?

Most people do not realize that the term "antichrist" is used only by the Apostle John, and only in his epistles. It occurs five times altogether, three times in chapter 2 of John's first epistle; once in chapter 4; and once in his second epistle. It appears from what is said in I John 2:18 that there will be a personal antichrist in the last days, though he is not sufficiently described for one to be positive which of the persons mentioned elsewhere in the prophetic scriptures is the one in view. Christian scholars do not all agree which personage is meant.

As to the thought of some particular living person being identified in this way, it must be remembered that the personal antichrist will not be revealed until the Tribulation period, when the prophecies relating to that time are being fulfilled. That time lies in the future, so we cannot identify any person living today as the antichrist.

The other references to the word *antichrist* show that in addition to describing the personal antichrist the word also refers to certain categories of persons. There were many persons in John's day, and have been ever since then, who fall into these categories.

The first use of the word occurs in I John 2:18, where we have two of the five occurrences. That verse says: "Little children, it is the last time: and as ye have heard that antichrist shall come, even now are there many antichrists; whereby we know that it is the last time." John does not here describe these antichrists, but makes it clear that many persons could be classified in that way.

What is said in verse 22, the third occurrence of the word, seems to describe the personal antichrist who shall be revealed in the last days. This verse says: "Who is a liar but he that denieth that Jesus is the Christ? He is antichrist, that denieth the Father and the Son." This verse should keep us from making foolish identifications, which many have done from time to time. The personal antichrist will not only deny that Jesus was the true Messiah but he will deny the truth of the Holy Trinity.

Some have thought this description corresponds with that found in Daniel 11:37: "Neither shall he regard the God of his fathers, nor the desire of women [the Messiah], nor regard any god: for he shall magnify himself above all." Yet the next verse says, "But in his estate [his exalted position] shall he honor the god of forces: and a god whom his fathers knew not shall he honor with gold, and silver, and with precious stones, and pleasant things." We find something similar to this in II Thessalonians 2:4: "Who opposeth and exalteth himself above all that is called God, or that is worshipped; so that he as God sitteth in the temple of God, showing himself that he is God." In view of the similarity of these passages some Bible scholars believe the same person is in view in Daniel 11:37; II Thessalonians 2:4; and I John 2:22.

Not only does I John 2:18 indicate that there are now many who can be called antichrists but we have two descriptions of them in I John 4:3 and II John verse 7. In the context of the first of these references believers are warned not to believe "every spirit," which means they are not to consider that every one who professes to speak for God has necessarily been sent by Him. He may be motivated by a different spirit. I John 4:3 says: "And every spirit that confesseth not that Jesus Christ is come in the flesh is not of God: and this is that spirit of antichrist, whereof ye have heard that it should come; and even now already is it in the world." Those versed in Bible study see in this an implication of antichrist's denial of Christ's deity and preexistence before His incarnation, as well as the actuality of His coming into the world in incarnation.

II John 7 takes this up again, "For many deceivers are entered into the world, who confess not that Jesus Christ is come in the flesh. This is a deceiver and an antichrist." Such persons are said in verse 9 *not* to abide in the doctrine of Christ, and those who follow their teaching are described as "having not God." We cannot be right with God the Father unless we give equal honor to His Son, as the Lord Jesus Himself said: "He that honoreth not the Son honoreth not the Father which hath sent him" (John 5:23). In the sense of these verses, many antichrists are in the world. However, the personal antichrist will appear only in the last days.

99. If "every eye" shall see Christ at His second coming, would not all submit to Him, and so be saved?

Christ's second coming to earth is described in Matthew 24 as being similar to flashing lightning. But lightning, while visible over a large area, is not visible throughout the earth. Revelation 1:7 says, "Behold, he cometh with clouds; and every eye shall see him, and they also which pierced him: and all kindreds of the earth shall wail because of him." This seems to refer to Zechariah 12:10-14, which clearly speaks of the nation of Israel.

The word *earth* in Revelation 1:7 can be translated "land," and the word *kindreds* can be translated "tribes." If the text is read with these alterations, it says, ". . . and all the tribes of the land shall wail because of him." With these changes, the text is brought into striking conformity to the reference in Zechariah 12, and suggests that the Lord's first visible revelation of Himself when He comes back to earth will be to those in the land of Palestine. And with those He will deal first, on the principle that "judgment must begin at the house of God" (I Pet. 4:17). Having dealt with those present in Palestine, the Lord will then present His claims to the rest of the inhabitants of the earth.

But those in Palestine will have been faced with His claims, and so He will deal with them on the ground of the attitude already shown. He will deal with the rest on the ground of their reaction to His claims presented by the messengers referred to in Isaiah 66:19, if we take that text to refer to that time.

100. Do chapters 17 and 18 of Revelation indicate that the city of Babylon will be rebuilt?

Scholars have been sharply divided as to whether these chapters refer to a literal city of Babylon or whether the use of the name in them is symbolic. Some take the view that the name is symbolic in chapter 17, but that in chapter 18 a literal city is meant. There can be little doubt that the reference in Revelation 17 is symbolic, since the name is recorded "MYSTERY, BABY-LON THE GREAT," and the description identifies it with the city of Rome.

Chapter 18 speaks of a literal city, but it is not equally clear whether it is to be identified with Babylon or Rome. Some scholars believe that the ancient city of Babylon has never experienced the utter desolation described in the prophecies of Ezekiel and Jeremiah, and therefore there will be a rebuilding of the city, to be followed by future desolations which will be in keeping with those prophecies. Others consider that the import of these prophecies has been fulfilled in the past history of Babylon, and that the references in Revelation 18 are to Rome, called Babylon because of its spiritual status, much as Jerusalem is called "Sodom" in Revelation 11:8. Where there is such diversity of view among Bible scholars, perhaps we shall have to await the event to clarify the import of the prophecy.

101. Are we to take Isaiah 11:6-9 literally?

The description given in these verses applies to the time of Christ's second advent, when, instead of coming in humility, He shall be manifested in power and great glory. At His first advent He made atonement for sin by His sufferings and death; at His second advent He shall remove the curse of sin from the physical world, including the animal creation. This will make the earth fruitful, and eliminate men's fears, so that there will be no excuse for men to sin.

The verses in question say: "The wolf also shall dwell with the lamb, and the leopard shall lie down with the kid; and the calf and the young lion and the fatling together; and a little child shall lead them. And the cow and the bear shall feed; their young ones shall lie down together; and the lion shall eat straw like the ox. And the sucking child shall play on the hole of the asp, and the weaned child shall put his hand on the cockatrice' den. They shall not hurt nor destroy in all my holy mountain: for the earth shall

be full of the knowledge of the LORD, as the waters cover the sea."
There is a similar passage in Isaiah 65, where the context indicates it also is to be taken literally. Romans 8:19-21 seems to refer
to this change in conditions in the world.

102. What is meant by the millennium?

The term "millennium" is simply the Latin for "a thousand
years." It is taken from Revelation 20, where six times the duration of Christ's earthly kingdom is said to be a thousand years.
But the word *millennium* has taken on a technical significance, as
representative of all that is said of Christ's earthly reign in other
passages as well. Hence today many persons speak of the "millennium," not so much signifying its duration of a thousand years but
a time or condition in which there shall be universal peace and
prosperity, because these things are prophesied of Christ's kingdom.

It would not be possible within a limited scope to refer to all
the passages relating to this kingdom. In the Old Testament far
more is said of that time than of Christ's first advent into the
world. Isaiah 2:4 and Micah 4:3 state that at that time "they shall
beat their swords into plowshares, and their spears into pruning-
hooks: nation shall not lift up sword against nation, neither shall
they learn war any more." At that time the curse of sin shall be
removed from the earth (Rom. 8:21), so that "instead of the thorn
shall come up the fir tree, and instead of the brier shall come up
the myrtle tree: and it shall be to the LORD for a name, for an
everlasting sign that shall not be cut off" (Isa. 55:13). Many other
prophecies tell of Christ ruling in righteousness, resulting in universal peace (Isa. 32:1, 17). This is usually what people have in
mind in speaking of the millennium.

103. Will children be born during the millennium?

From my understanding of prophecy, I would say yes. Scriptures referring to that period speak of children, indicating that

there will be births during the millennium. The curse is to be removed from the earth, making it more fruitful. It appears also that human life shall be greatly extended, for we read in Isaiah 65:22: ". . . as the days of a tree are the days of my people, and mine elect shall long enjoy the work of their hands."

However, such longevity does not necessarily involve glorified bodies, as will be true of those who shall inhabit heaven. It means that the law of death which works in our bodies now will be overcome by the changed condition of the earth and its surroundings. Students of the Bible have long noticed that before the time of the flood, men lived many hundred of years, the longest-lived being Methuselah, whose age was 969. It is believed that conditions in the millennium will be such that long life will be universal except for those who are killed under the judgment of God. And since human bodies will not then be in the glorified state, births will be the natural outcome, and these—as in the early days—will probably be spaced at far greater intervals.

104. What is meant by a child dying at a hundred years old (in Isaiah 65:20) and a sinner being accursed at that age?

The passage is a prophecy concerning conditions that will prevail during the millennial kingdom of Christ. In the first part of this verse, we read: "There shall be no more thence an infant of days, nor an old man that hath not lived out his days." We take this to mean that during this period no one shall die in infancy, nor will anyone die of old age, since the span of life will be greatly increased, and medicine will be available for any illness (Rev. 22:2).

One who shall die at the age of 100 at that time will be considered to have died as a child. But this age (100 years) apparently will be the age of accountability, since "the sinner being a hundred years old shall be accursed." This confirms the fact that then death will not be from what we now call "natural causes," but will be the result of the judgment of God. Psalm 101:8 has been rendered, "Morning by morning I will destroy all the wicked of the land, that I may cut off all wicked doers from the city of the LORD." This has been taken to mean that every morning there will be summary judgment of all wickedness since, under conditions which shall exist then, there will be no incentive to sin. It seems that one who commits a transgression will have until the following morning to repent and make the matter right.

105. What is meant by the words "this generation" in Matthew 24:34 ("This generation shall not pass till all these things be fulfilled")?

The expression "this generation" has been taken by some to mean a race or a people marked by certain moral characteristics. This would mean that the unbelieving generation which rejected the Lord Jesus would continue until Christ's second coming. Though scattered, they would not lose their national identity in that sense.

Others believe that "this generation" means the generation of persons living when Christ spoke these words, since many of that generation were alive when the destruction of Jerusalem was accomplished. This was true, but the problem with that view is that the Lord had spoken not only of the destruction of Jerusalem but also of His own return to earth in glory; and that part of the prophecy has not been fulfilled.

A third view seems more acceptable. It is that the generation which sees the beginning of the final fulfillment of the prophecies uttered by the Lord will see the consummation of those prophecies. This does not mean that we can set a date for the time of our Lord's coming, which we are told no man knows (Mark 13:32). We have no way of knowing from what event we should begin the counting of the generation, nor are we told the precise length of the generation. But the implication is that when these events begin to take place, they will reach their completion in a swift succession of events.

106. If Israel was God's earthly people, does this mean that in the resurrection believing Israelites will be restored to the earth?

We believe not. We read in Hebrews 11:13-17 that Abraham, and presumably other patriarchs, desired "a better country, that is, an heavenly: wherefore God is not ashamed to be called their God: for he hath prepared for them a city." This verse, it seems to me, indicates that those who died in faith will be resurrected with the Church, and will share in the heavenly Jerusalem. The names of the twelve tribes of the children of Israel are said to be on the gates of that city, though the significance of this is not stated, and could be explained in various ways.

The first resurrection is described in I Corinthians 15:23 as including those "that are Christ's at his coming." This, it seems to me, includes Old Testament believers, as well as New Testament ones. I Thessalonians 4:16 is similar, for it speaks of the raising of "the dead in Christ." I take it that the earthly promises to Israel will be fulfilled to those who are living on the earth during the millennial kingdom of Christ. I do not see in the Bible any suggestion that any person, raised from the dead, is placed back on the earth, except in those cases where resurrection followed shortly after death, and was a renewal and, in a sense, a prolongation of their earthly life. But resurrection, according to Philippians 3:20-21, involves glorification of the body.

107. If Old Testament believers are to be in the heavenly city in the resurrection, and are not part of the body and bride of Christ, what will be their relationship to Him?

We believe that their relationship was described by John the Baptist, when he said, "Ye yourselves bear me witness, that I said, I am not the Christ, but that I am sent before him. He that hath the bride is the bridegroom: but the friend of the bridegroom, which standeth and heareth him, rejoiceth greatly because of the bridegroom's voice: this my joy therefore is fulfilled. He must increase, but I must decrease" (John 3:28-30).

In these statements John identified the Bridegroom, the bride, and the friends of the Bridegroom. The fact that he classified himself as a "friend of the bridegroom" suggests that this might be the relationship of the Old Testament believers to Christ—a relationship which differs from that of the Church, which is declared, in Ephesians 5, to be the body and bride of Christ. Revelation 19:7 speaks of the marriage of the Lamb, and verse 9 adds, "Blessed are they which are called unto the marriage supper of the Lamb." It seems more appropriate to apply this verse to the friends of the Bridegroom rather than to the bride.

108. What is meant by "the future judgment"?

Many judgments are mentioned in the Bible. Some of them relate to individuals, and some to particular nations. When we speak of "future judgment," most people think of the final judgment of God on all those who have died in their sins, not having received Christ by faith as their Saviour and not acknowledging His claims.

This final judgment is described in Revelation 20:11-15, but it is not, as many think, a judgment to decide whether people are saved or lost. That is determined before we die. Ephesians 2:3 tells us that "we were by nature children of wrath," and Jesus said, as recorded in John 3:18, "He that believeth on him [the Son] is not condemned: but he that believeth not is condemned already, because he hath not believed in the name of the only begotten Son of God."

The judgment described in Revelation 20 is to determine the *measure* of each person's guilt, and hence is based on the record of their works, represented by the "books" which were opened. The book of life is opened as a negative witness, showing that their names are *not* written in it. Believers in Christ will not be found in that judgment, since Christ bore their sins in His body and put them away by the sacrifice of Himself. "There is therefore now no condemnation to them which are in Christ Jesus" (Rom. 8:1). John 5:24 says believers "shall not come into condemnation [judgment]."

109. Does the Bible mention a time when all men will be reconciled to God?

The Bible makes it very plain that all men will *not* be saved, because it speaks of the lost in hell enduring endless grief. The Lord Jesus indicated this in Luke 16:19-31, where the rich man who died unsaved was promised no relief, but was told instead that there was no escape from the place of torment where he was. Many other scriptures confirm this, and while the "fire" mentioned may be figurative, the torment is clearly taught. The Lord Jesus spoke of it as "weeping, and wailing, and gnashing of teeth."

A mistaken idea is often drawn from Colossians 1:20 through failure to recognize that the word *all* is usually limited by the context in which it is used. When Caesar issued a decree that "all the world should be taxed" (Luke 2:1), the word *all* referred to *his* world. When God loved the world and gave His Son to be our Saviour, this means all of *God's* world, the whole human race.

In speaking of reconciliation to God, the Apostle Paul limited this to "things in earth" and "things in heaven" (Col. 1:20). There is a significant omission in this verse, for when the apostle spoke of the subjugation of mankind in Philippians 2:10 he mentioned "things in heaven, and things on earth, and things under the earth." The lost in hell will be forced to bow in submission to Christ, but it is not said that they will be reconciled; and the gnashing of teeth of which the Lord spoke may well indicate this. But those on the redeemed earth in the eternal state will be reconciled, as well as those inhabiting the heavens.

110. How does the United States fit into Bible prophecy?

Some students of the Bible believe that certain references in prophecy to far-off places point to the United States, without identifying it. Those taking this view have difficulty in assigning a specific role to the United States in the prophetical scheme. Others, who identify the harlot of Revelation 17 with apostate Christendom, consider that the expression "mother of harlots" implies that wherever Christianity is professed, especially where it is the predominant religion of a country, such countries are included in the prophecy. If that be so, then what is said of "Babylon the Great" in Revelation 17 and 18 would apply to the countries of North and South America, since the predominant religion of those countries is Christianity. We do not mean that all are believers, but that this is the acknowledged religion of the great majority of the inhabitants.

However, others do not see in the prophetical utterances any specific reference to any great political or military power in the West. These take it that, at the time when these prophecies will be fulfilled, there will not be such a power. One commentator says that the United States, which came into the place of leadership comparatively quickly, could subside even more quickly. One writer on political science, without reference to Scripture, also came to the conclusion that the elements which made the United States strong during its struggles would operate to the opposite result after she became strong, causing weakness and loss of leadership.

HEAVEN AND HELL

111. When an Old Testament saint died, did he go directly to heaven or to some other place? If he did not go into the presence of Christ, is he there now?

Statements concerning life after death in the Old Testament are not precise. In II Timothy 1:9, 10 we read, "Who hath saved us, and called us with an holy calling, not according to our works, but according to his own purpose and grace, which was given us in Christ Jesus before the world began, but is now made manifest by the appearing of our Saviour Jesus Christ, who hath abolished [or, nullified] death, and hath brought life and immortality [incorruptibility] to light through the gospel." For these things to be fully revealed and understood required the advent of Christ and the fulfilling of the work of atonement.

In the Old Testament the dead were said to go to *sheol*, the equivalent of the New Testament *hades*. This word simply refers to the unseen world which the spirits of those who died entered. It does not distinguish the destiny of the saved from that of the lost. The Lord Jesus did distinguish their destiny when He told, as recorded in Luke 16, of two men who died. Both were in hades (the unseen world), but both had conscious existence. However, though in hades, they were not in the same locality, nor in the same company.

The saved one was said to be in Abraham's bosom, a figure for being in his fellowship. It was a place of comfort, and since Abraham is called "the father of all them that believe" (Rom. 4:11), those who died in faith are said to have gone to be with him. Christ was not yet glorified as a man, and it was not meet that they should be in the presence of the divine glory before sin

119

was actually put away. It was forgiven in anticipation of Christ's atonement. Now that the work of atonement is completed and Christ is glorified, believers who die are no longer said to be with Abraham but to "be with Christ which is far better" (Phil. 1:23).

The unsaved man of Luke 16 was already in a place of torment, even though he still awaits the judgment of the Great White Throne, for that judgment determines the degree of suffering, just as the "judgment seat of Christ" determines the reward of the believer. But the fact of being saved or lost is determined now by our attitude to Christ, as we read in John 3:18.

We are not told the precise position of those who were said to be with Abraham, but we read in Hebrews 12:23 of "the spirits of just men made perfect." My own opinion is that while they were in heaven, there may have been some kind of veil separating them from the immediate presence or recognition of God Himself, until Christ ascended as a glorified Man to take His seat at God's right hand.

112. What scriptures show that a believer goes to be with the Lord immediately after death?

A number of scriptures teach this. One would be Luke 24:23, where we read our Lord's words of assurance to the thief who turned to Him in faith on the cross: "Verily I say unto thee, To day shalt thou be with me in paradise" (Luke 23:43). Some contend that this should be read, "Verily I say unto thee today," but this would be unnatural, and would leave the Lord's remark a vague statement.

See also our Lord's account of the rich man and Lazarus. As soon as Lazarus died he "was carried by the angels into Abraham's bosom" (Luke 16:22).

When Paul was contemplating the possibility of death, at his first imprisonment, he said, in Philippians 1:21-23, "For me to live is Christ, and to die is gain . . . having a desire to depart, and to be with Christ; which is far better. . . ."

Another plain doctrinal statement is found in II Corinthians

5:6-8, "Therefore we are always confident, knowing that, whilst we are at home in the body, we are absent from the Lord: (for we walk by faith, not by sight:) we are confident, I say, and willing rather to be absent from the body, and to be present with the Lord."

I believe each of these scriptures, and all of them together, warrant the belief that when a believer dies, he or she goes at once to be with the Lord.

113. Does a believer who dies and goes to be with Christ know those who have gone before?

I do not know of any doctrinal statement concerning this, but it seems to me it is implied in what is revealed of the state of the dead. In the story of the rich man and Lazarus, in Luke 16, they knew one another; also those with Jesus on the Mount of Transfiguration knew one another, even though they had never met Moses and Elijah, who are identified in each of the accounts not only by the writers of the Gospel records but also by those present on the mount.

There is every reason to believe that in the spirit world people recognize not only those whom they knew on earth but everyone else there. This may be part of the meaning of I Corinthians 13:12, "Then shall I know, even as also I am known." The word *know* is in a form which means "to know fully." I know of no basis for thinking we shall lose our powers of perception; rather, they would be enhanced. The rich man in hell was told to "remember," and perhaps he would have liked to forget. But for the believer remembering will give occasion for praise and thanksgiving to God.

114. Do those who have gone to be with Christ know what is going on here on earth?

So far as I understand the Bible, those in heaven do not know what is taking place on earth. It would be difficult to see how those in heaven would have peace if they saw members of their families living in sin on earth. We read, in Luke 16, of the rich man being concerned about his five brothers on earth, but this seems to relate to what he remembered of them. There is no suggestion that he saw what they were doing at that time.

That the dead do not know what is happening on earth seems to me to be the force of the statement in Ecclesiastes 9:5, ". . . the dead know not anything, neither have they any more a reward; for the memory of them is forgotten." This is not saying, as some people teach, that the dead know nothing where they are, but rather, I take it, that they no longer know, nor have any portion in, what is taking place on the earth. Heaven is not a projection of earth; it is an entirely different sphere. While we shall know one another there, those now living cannot communicate with those who have already died, nor are the dead any longer concerned with life on this earth.

115. Will all people in heaven be the same age, or will they be old or young, according to the age at which they die?

This question is asked most often by persons who have lost children in death in their infancy, and it is a question which reflects very poignant emotions. Another question often asked is whether persons who become physically decrepit due to advanced age will be in this state forever.

So far as we know, the Bible does not give an explicit answer to this question as it relates to children, but it does give some hints which will give us some ideas about it.

In I Corinthians 15, beginning at verse 42, we are told that the resurrection body will be different from our present body. We are told that the body "is sown in corruption; it is raised in incorruption: it is sown in dishonor; it is raised in glory: it is sown in weakness; it is raised in power: it is sown a natural [or, soulish] body; it is raised a spiritual body [or, a body suited to the spirit]." These verses show clearly that we shall not carry any physical defects into heaven. Whatever disabilities the body may suffer in this life, they will be completely corrected and overcome in the resurrection.

But while these verses assure us there will be no physical defects in anyone in heaven, they say nothing about age correspondence. As to this, I know of nothing specific, but some have thought that what is said in I John 3:2 is relevant. There we read, "Beloved, now are we the sons of God, and it doth not yet appear what we shall be: but we know that when he shall appear, we shall be like him; for we shall see him as he is." Christ died at the age of thirty-three in the full vigor of manhood.

Many think that in addition to the removal of physical defects, everyone will be restored to a youthful state, so that all who are in heaven will be there in full vigor. If this be true, and it seems to me to be in keeping with what Scripture says about the resurrection, then is it not likely that infants will be there as immature persons. They would not experience any "growing up" in heaven, since their infant bodies will not be taken to heaven without having been transformed. Part of the fruit of Christ's redemption will be this: that all who go to heaven will share in physical perfection there.

116. Shall we be reunited with our loved ones in heaven? How could we be happy there if some members of our family were not saved?

It is difficult for many persons to think of heaven as being anything other than a projection of our life here. Consequently they anticipate a resumption of family fellowship, especially where this has been happy.

One person wrote, "My husband and I find our greatest agreement on spiritual matters. We have seven beautiful youngsters, the first three of which are already saved. Is such a relationship to be considered part of the chaff to be burned up at the end of time?" It isn't chaff, but I believe it is for earth, and not for heaven.

What about families which are not united in Christ? Shall they spend eternity denied forever the joy others would have in hav-

ing united families? And what about families where a husband
or wife has died, and there has been a second marriage, sometimes with children by both marriages? For myself, I do not believe there will be any broken families in heaven, for we shall be
there as the family of God.

The Bible encourages, and even commands, love between members of earthly families. But we must ever be conscious of the
fact that Christ is both the Source and Object of our *deepest* joy
and blessing. Sometimes when a loved one is taken away in
death, the lives of those left behind are shattered, as though
Christ has no consolation sufficient to make up for the loss of a
loved one. Certainly we miss them, and mourn their loss. Scripture has no criticism of this. But if Christ can satisfy our hearts
only if the members of our family are included, then we un-
wittingly are failing to give Him the place of supremacy in our
hearts which He deserves. How then could a person find satis-
faction in heaven whose family were not with him there?

I Corinthians 15:44 tells us that in heaven our bodies will be
entirely different in their nature, and in Luke 20:35-36 the Lord
Jesus tells us that the marriage relationship has no place there.
No doubt we shall know one another and be able to rejoice together in the memories of God's grace to us.

II Corinthians 5:16, it seems to me, sheds significant light on
this question: "Henceforth know we no man after the flesh: yea,
though we have known Christ after the flesh, yet now henceforth
know we him no more." If in heaven those who knew Christ
after the flesh will not be nearer to Him than those who love
Him without having previously seen Him (I Pet. 1:8), I am quite
sure that our earthly relationships among ourselves will not be
the basis of our joy in heaven.

117. Does Revelation 19:11-14 indicate there will be animals in heaven?

These verses speak of the second coming of Christ at the head
of the armies of heaven. Both Christ and those who follow Him
are said to ride on white horses. It seems clear that this is figura-

tive language, since in the description given, these ride from heaven to earth. In the Bible we find no suggestion of earthly animals in heaven, and if the animals referred to in these verses (horses) are to be taken literally, it would be creatures whose origin is heaven. However, I think the language is figurative.

Many who have become very much attached to various animal pets feel there must be a provision for them in heaven. But such a conception assumes that heaven is a projection of earth, which we believe is a fallacy. Besides, we are distinctly taught in Scripture that brute beasts are "made to be taken and destroyed" (II Pet. 2:12). This teaching does not countenance any torturing of animals, but it does justify the taking of animal life to provide food for man, as we are told in Genesis 9:1-3.

The Lord Jesus makes it clear in Matthew 10:28, as well as in other passages, that a human being continues in conscious existence after death. This truth is developed more fully in Luke 20:27-38. Nothing like this is said of any animal. Man is said to be made in the image of God, something that is never affirmed of any anmial. We believe it is a dishonor to God to equate human life with that of animals. The entire Book of Revelation contains many figurative expressions, and we take it that the words *horse* and *horses* in these verses are used in a figurative sense. We know of no reason why anyone in a resurrected glorified body would require the use of a horse.

118. What is the need for resurrection, since we go to heaven or hell at death?

We understand from I Thessalonians 5:23 that man is a tripartite being, consisting of spirit and soul and body. This is one of the ways in which he is made in the likeness of God, since God is a triune God, and although the parallel is not perfect, it helps us to understand the nature of God's being. Man would not be a complete being, if his body were not raised. Just as sin has pervaded man's entire being, so the redemption which Christ has wrought applies to man in the entirety of his being.

With regard to going to heaven or hell at death, it is true that the believer is said to go to be "with Christ, which is far better" (Phil. 1:23), but this does not mean that he at once receives the rewards he may have earned in Christian service. Such rewards will be given at the judgment seat of Christ, which will take place immediately after the resurrection of believers described in I Thessalonians 4:13-18.

Likewise, although those who die unsaved go at once to a place of torment, as the Lord Jesus indicated in Luke 16, yet they also await the final appraisal of their lives after their resurrection, mentioned in Revelation 20, when they enter into the final phase of their condemnation. The judgment of unbelievers, like the reward of believers, will be based on the record of their lives, as this chapter shows. Meantime, it is the spirit and soul which are in heaven or hades, and not the body. In eternity, each person will be complete by reason of the resurrection of the body.

HOLY SPIRIT

119. Can we show from the Bible that the Holy Spirit is a person and not merely an influence or power? Also, can we prove His deity?

God is a spirit. However, this statement does not deny that He is a personal God. Although the Holy Spirit is symbolized in Scripture by *wind, breath, fire,* and *water,* He is nevertheless revealed as a person. Foreknowledge is ascribed to Him in the Bible, which also states that He was sent into the world on a mission from God the Father and the Son. We are told that the Holy Spirit can be grieved, and His power quenched. Also, He is said to be the One who reveals God. None of these statements could be made about abstract power.

Besides, the Holy Spirit is said to be God, and this could not be said about what is only an attribute of God. In Acts 5:3 Peter said Ananias lied to the Holy Ghost, while in verse 4 Ananias is told that he lied to God. Thus the Holy Spirit is clearly called God. In II Corinthians 3:17 the Holy Spirit is given the title "Lord," the equivalent of the name "Jehovah" in the Old Testament. This is a divine name, given to each of the persons of the Holy Trinity.

The deity and personality of the Holy Spirit are also emphasized by the association, in the Bible, of His name with that of the Father and of the Son on an equality which could not be accorded any created being. We have examples of this in the formula for baptism ("In the name of the Father, and of the Son, and of the Holy Spirit") as well as in the benediction of II Corinthians 3:17, and elsewhere. Lewis S. Chafer notes in his *Systematic Theology* that all three primary names for God—Elohim, Jehovah, and

127

Adonai—are used of each of the persons of the Godhead: Father,
Son, and Holy Spirit.

120. Does the command in Ephesians 5:18 to be "filled with the Spirit" mean we must receive more of the Holy Spirit?

I believe not. I take this verse to mean that we should be so
completely yielded to the Holy Spirit that He can possess us fully
and, in that sense, fill us. He is a person, and is not given by measure. The Holy Spirit dwells within every believer (Rom. 8:9;
Eph. 1:13-14), but He can be grieved (Eph. 4:30), and His activity within us can be quenched (I Thess. 5:19). When we allow
this to happen we do not experience the fullness of the Holy Spirit's working and power in and through us.

To be filled with the Spirit implies freedom for Him to occupy
every part of our life, guiding and controlling us. Then His power
can be exerted through us, so that what we do is fruitful to God.
But this filling does not only apply to outward acts; it applies
equally to our inmost thoughts and motives. When we are
filled with the Spirit, all is subject to His control. Psalm 19:14
says, "Let the words of my mouth, and *the meditation of my heart*,
be acceptable in thy sight, O LORD, my strength, and my re-
deemer."

There is another sense in which the Holy Spirit comes upon a
person, giving him power for a particular activity. We read, in the
Old Testament especially, of the Holy Spirit coming upon a person to empower him to accomplish certain exploits. There may be
a parallel to this in Acts 4:31. There we read that when the assembled disciples had prayed, "the place was shaken where they
were assembled together; and they were all filled with the Holy
Ghost, and they spake the word of God with boldness." There is
no more conflict between the Holy Spirit's dwelling in us and His
coming upon us in this special way than there is between the fact
of God's omnipresence and our drawing near to Him in prayer.
But we cannot expect the Holy Spirit to fill us for service if we do
not allow Him to fill us in the personal way already mentioned.

121. Is it right or necessary to pray for the power of the Holy Spirit to be exercised in us, since every believer is indwelt by the Holy Spirit in this dispensation?

The indwelling presence of the Holy Spirit is the mark or seal that we belong to God, that we are His children by faith in Jesus Christ. However His presence is not a guarantee that we shall live a spiritual or fruitful life. We learn from Ephesians 4:30 that it is possible for the believer to grieve the Holy Spirit. This has the effect of quenching the Spirit (I Thess. 5:19). We believe that the manifestation of His power in our lives is dependent on our so yielding ourselves to Him that He is free to use us. Then His power will be operative in what we do for Christ.

But this may also require the exercise of prayer, and perhaps this is the meaning of Luke 11:13: "How much more shall your heavenly Father give the Holy Spirit to them that ask him?" This has been explained as having reference to the time before Pentecost. But the indwelling presence of the Holy Spirit was never a subject of prayer. According to John 7:39, the giving of the Holy Spirit in the sense of an indwelling presence awaited the glorification of the Lord Jesus. He was not given to indwell believers before Pentecost, whether they prayed or not; and after Pentecost, He was said to indwell all believers as the Seal which marked them as belonging to God (Eph. 1:13-14).

But it should be noticed that in the original text of Luke 11:13 there is not the definite article before the words "Holy Spirit." This means that it is not His person that is in view in this text but rather His gifts and power. This is confirmed by the fact that the parallel passage, Matthew 7:11, reads "give good things" instead of "give the Holy Spirit." It would seem, then, that if we are not grieving, and thus quenching, the Holy Spirit, it is appropriate for us to pray that His power may be manifested in our life and service for Christ.

122. How is the ministry of the Holy Spirit different in this dispensation from His previous ministry?

The answer is given by the Lord Jesus in John 14:16-17: "And I will pray the Father, and he shall give you another Comforter, that he may abide with you for ever; even the Spirit of truth; whom the world cannot receive, because it seeth him not, neither knoweth him: but ye know him; for he dwelleth with you, and shall be in you." The chief distinction seems to be His indwelling presence in each believer, though the ramifications of this stupendous fact are many.

In Ephesians 1:13-14 we are told that we are "sealed with that Holy Spirit of promise, which is the earnest of our inheritance until the redemption of the purchased possession, unto the praise of his glory." The "seal" marks us out as God's property, and gives us the assurance of eternal salvation. Old Testament believers were just as safe, for their salvation rested on the same basis as ours, but they did not have the divine assurance which is given us in the Word of God, and confirmed by the indwelling presence of the Holy Spirit.

He is also "the earnest of our inheritance." The "earnest" in times past was both a sample and a pledge. This means, then, that He dwells in us not only passively but actively, making relevant in our lives the precious truths of God's Word concerning us. They become a present reality, by His grace and power. We are told elsewhere in the Bible that Christ's atoning work now makes us "sons" in God's household, and it is the Holy Spirit who enables us to enjoy and experience the privileges which go with that sonship.

123. How can I know whether the many things I have heard about the Holy Spirit's relationship to believers in Christ are true of me?

Some of the things said about the Holy Spirit's relationship to the believer are true of *all* believers. We can be sure, on the authority of God's Word, that all such statements are true of us if we are true believers in Christ.

For example, I John 5:1 says, "Whosoever believeth that Jesus is the Christ is born of God." Since the new birth is by the Holy Spirit, we can be sure, if we are true believers in the Lord Jesus, that we have been "born again." There will be additional evidences of this, but our basic authority for claiming the new birth on the basis of faith in Christ, is what God says in His Word.

Also, the Holy Spirit dwells in each believer. Romans 8:9 says, "But ye are not in the flesh, but in the Spirit, if so be that the Spirit of God dwell in you. Now if any man have not the Spirit of Christ, he is none of his." This is the plainest possible declaration that each believer is indwelt by the Holy Spirit. Ephesians 1:13 tells us that the presence of the Holy Spirit is the divine seal indicating that we belong to God: "in whom also, after that ye believed [or, having believed], ye were sealed with that holy Spirit of promise." The next verse adds, "Which is the earnest of our inheritance until the redemption of the purchased possession, unto the praise of his glory."

That is to say, having believed on Christ, we are born of the Spirit, and also indwelt by Him, who not only marks us out as children of God, but makes good in our experience that portion of the promises of God which is intended to apply to the present time. As the "earnest of our inheritance" the indwelling Spirit is the pledge of the future complete fulfillment of God's promises concerning us and of present empowerment for Christian living. He is also the "anointing" mentioned in II Corinthians 1:21-22 and I John 2:20, 27. The coming of the Holy Spirit upon believers is an anointing, as was true of His coming upon the Lord Jesus (Luke 4:18; Acts 10:38).

Another thing which is true of every believer is described in I Corinthians 12:13: "By one Spirit are we all baptized into one body, whether we be Jews or Gentiles, whether we be bond or free, and have been all made to drink into one Spirit." I Corinthians 1:2 shows that this epistle was addressed to "all that in every place call upon the name of Jesus Christ our Lord, both theirs and ours."

All of these relationships with the Holy Spirit are assured to every child of God on the authority of God's Word.

124. Does Ephesians 4:5 teach that the baptism of the Holy Spirit has displaced water baptism?

From the words "one Lord, one faith, one baptism" in Ephesians 4:5, some have inferred that the baptism of the Holy Spirit is the only baptism for believers in this dispensation. We do not believe this is the import of the text, even though this verse be taken to refer to the baptism of the Holy Spirit, a position which I do not take. If the word *baptism* refers to water baptism, it would mean one of two things: (1) that the rite of baptism is performed once in a person's experience, or (2) that water baptism is the almost universally accepted mark of Christian profession.

That God intended water baptism to be practiced in this dispensation seems clear to me from the fact that our Lord's post-resurrection ministry included the command to His disciples to baptize, plus the fact that baptism was practiced in the early church. In the case of the household of Cornelius, not only is water baptism specified but the command to submit to this rite was based on the fact that they had already given evidence of having received the gift of the Holy Spirit (Acts 10:44-48). We see nothing in Scripture to indicate the discontinuance of this practice, nor do we see any ground for relating all references to baptism in the epistles to the baptism of the Holy Spirit.

125. Can a person be saved without the baptism of the Spirit?

We believe not, for the simple reason that we are told in I Corinthians 12:13 that "by one Spirit are we all baptized into one body." This epistle was addressed not only to all the believers in Corinth but also to "all that in every place call upon the name of Jesus Christ our Lord" (1:2). The baptism of the Spirit is not described as an experience subsequent to believing the gospel, nor is it predicated upon any other condition than believing the gospel. Consequently, every true believer is baptized by (or, in) the Spirit and thus united to the body of Christ. No believer is left out of this experience, so it is not possible to be saved without it.

PRAYER

126. What are the conditions on which God will answer prayer?

In the Bible we find numerous conditions which believers must meet if they are to receive the petitions they ask of God. These conditions can be placed in two categories: (1) The thing we ask for must be in His will for us. (2) We must be in a right relationship with God; we must be on what someone has called "praying ground." While there are many places in the Bible where these conditions are not mentioned, they are implied, since they are given elsewhere in the Bible. I believe it is wrong to take a general statement such as is found in John 14:14 and claim it as a promise without considering other conditions. There Christ said, "If ye shall ask anything in my name, I will do it."

I John 5:14-15 clearly states that acceptable prayer must be "according to his [God's] will," and James 4:3 says, "Ye ask, and receive not, because ye ask amiss, that ye may consume it upon your lusts." I John 3:20-22 makes it clear that our hearts must be right with God. James 1:5-7 shows that our asking must be in faith, in keeping with our Lord's words in Mark 11:24, "What things soever ye desire, when ye pray, believe that ye receive them, and ye shall have them."

The verses which follow that promise of Christ show that we must have a forgiving spirit toward others. These verses do not refer to salvation but to the believer's communion with God. It is broken if we harbor an unforgiving spirit toward others. The parables of Luke 11 and 18 show that we must be urgent and persistent in our praying.

There are other instructions concerning prayer, but the verses here referred to represent the major ones.

127. Since we believe a Christian's life is planned by the Lord, why do we pray for a believer when sickness comes? Do our prayers cause God to pay more attention to this one?

We agree that the believer's life is planned by the Lord, and that He allows sicknesses to come. Such things are a discipline, not only for the person who becomes sick but for all others in the Christian group (I Cor. 12:26). The person is cast on the Lord for restoration of health, and others are exercised in sympathy to do what they can for the person involved. All of these exercises help to keep us all close to the Lord.

We believe that when the Lord permits sickness to come, it is not ordinarily intended to be a permanent condition, although sometimes a person contracts an incurable disease. But God has put within the body tremendous powers of healing. He has also put in the world a wide variety of things which can help and hasten the healing and restoring processes. And especially in late years, God has enabled men to learn the proper use of such drugs. We believe it is as much in order to make a proper use of these as to make a proper use of food to sustain the body.

In praying for a sick person we are acknowledging to God our concern for the person, and our dependence upon Him to bring about restoration of health in the person. As with other forms of prayer, God has made His intervention dependent on our praying. "Ask, and it shall be given you" (Matt. 7:7). "Ye have not because ye ask not" (James 4:2).

128. Is it correct to say "Prayer changes things"? Can prayer change God's purposes?

It would be more accurate to say that "God changes things in answer to prayer." Sometimes people get the idea that in some mystical way prayer operates by a power of its own. Rather, prayer is making our requests known to God, and in answering prayer, God acts on our behalf to alter circumstances.

I would not say that our prayers cause God to alter His plans or purposes. God has made many of His promises dependent on our prayers. He does not automatically give everything to us. The Lord Jesus said, "Ask, and it shall be given you; seek, and ye shall find . . ." (Matt. 7:7). In Matthew 9:29, after some dialogue with the blind men who desired to receive their sight, Jesus said, "According to your faith be it unto you."

It should be understood that God knew all He would do "from the beginning of the world" (Acts 15:18), but He formulated His plans on the basis of foreknowing also all our actions and reactions. It does not require any change in God to answer our prayers, but He would have planned differently had He foreseen that we would not pray in a given circumstance. God permits our cooperation with Him in the ministry of prayer.

129. How should we teach young children to pray? Can a child five or six years old be truly saved?

Some parents teach young children to use a form of prayer or to recite a stanza of a hymn, especially if it is in the form of a prayer. Others encourage their children to pray whatever is on their minds. The first method can lead to formalism, but not necessarily. The second, from my observation, can lead to more serious difficulties. Sometimes childish prayers go far afield. Frequently such prayers are considered by adults to be "cute" or "clever." I doubt very much the desirability of such "praying." If the child learns simply to ask God's blessing on home and family and to pray for daily needs, I think this can be helpful.

With regard to the salvation of little children, we must remember the great differences in individual children. Some mature earlier than others. Some children have professed conversion to Christ at five or six years of age, and have shown by a long and consistently godly life that they were truly saved. We cannot deny the possibility of very young children making a genuine commitment to Christ in faith.

On the other hand, some have made profession at even later ages, around ten to twelve, and yet when they became sixteen to eighteen their lives seemed more inspired by the devil than by

Christ. Some of such persons are recovered to their earlier profession but some are not.

I do not know of any way we can be sure a child is saved. If a
child makes a profession of faith in Christ, try to build on it, but
do not assume that every childish profession is necessarily the
result of the conviction of the Holy Spirit.

**130. Does God ever hear the prayers of unsaved persons? In
John 9:31 we read, "Now we know that God heareth not
sinners; but if any man be a worshipper of God, him he
heareth."**

It should be noticed that the words quoted were spoken by a
blind man who had just been given sight by the Lord Jesus. The
Pharisees were intent upon proving that Jesus was a sinner because He had performed this miracle on the sabbath day. The
man who had been blind considered it a self-evident truth that
"God heareth not sinners." He was not speaking as a prophet, by
divine revelation or inspiration.

Ordinarily, what the man said is true. God's promises concerning prayer have been given to His children. There are conditions
which must be met if one expects God to hear and answer prayer,
even when one is a believer. But when the prescribed conditions
are met, God will answer the prayers of His children, according
to His promises. No such promises are given to unbelievers.

But we must remember that God "maketh his sun to rise on the
evil and on the good, and sendeth rain on the just and on the unjust" (Matt. 5:45). And from Luke 6:35 we learn that God is
"kind unto the unthankful and to the evil." In view of this, we
cannot say that God never answers the prayers of unsaved persons, even though He is not pledged to do so. Psalm 72:12 says,
"He shall deliver the needy when he crieth, the poor also, and
him that hath no helper."

From the Scriptures it would appear that God often responds to
a cry for help, but it is less likely that He would answer interces-
sory prayers offered by unsaved persons. However, we can never
limit God, and He often shows grace where we would not.

131. Should not prayer be specific? How can general prayers be answered?

We do not believe the effectiveness of praying depends on particular features of the prayers themselves, other than their being in the will of God. It is rather a question of the state of the one who prays, in his relationship to God. Ordinarily, we believe that prayers should be specific, yet we are instructed in Scripture to engage in some praying which is not specific. For instance, in I Timothy 2:1-2 the Apostle Paul wrote, "I exhort therefore, that, . . . supplications, prayers, intercessions, and giving of thanks, be made for all men; for kings, and for all that are in authority; that we may lead a quiet and peaceable life in all godliness and honesty." "All men" is as general as any term could be; and while "kings, and all that are in authority" is more specific it can hardly be classified as a specific request. Yet verse 3 says, "For this is good and acceptable in the sight of God our Saviour."

The general and specific are combined in Ephesians 6:18-19: "Praying always with all prayer and supplication in the Spirit, . . . with all perseverance and supplication for all saints; and for me, . . . that I may open my mouth boldly, to make known the mystery of the gospel." Instructions to pray for people generally would not have been given if such prayer did not have value. Yet some persons pray *only* in general terms. But needs are often very specific, and I believe we ought to pray for people by name, and for particular needs. This constitutes a prayer ministry, and enables us to share the burdens of work which God has given others to do. In praying for all men, or people in a certain country or category, we ought to obtain as much information about them as possible, so that our hearts will be really burdened about their needs and their welfare. Then we can be sure that our prayers on their behalf will not be without value.

132. Why do we close our eyes when we pray? Also, is it necessary to kneel when we pray?

The Bible doesn't say we should close our eyes when we pray, but we believe that ordinarily it is proper to do so. Usually a speaker looks at the one to whom he is speaking, but when we speak to God, we close our eyes. To look at someone else, or to look around, would be, in these circumstances, irreverent. But there are times when a person cannot safely close his eyes—for instance, when he prays while driving a car. In addition to special prayer which may be required by the exigencies of driving, many use the time to commune with God about their own needs or those of others. In such a case, to have one's eyes open is not a sign of irreverence.

A prominent Christian leader said that when he prayed with his eyes closed he had a tendency to fall asleep. Also, when he kneeled for a long time, he felt uncomfortable, and this distracted him from praying. He overcame these difficulties by keeping his eyes open and walking about his room, while he prayed aloud using a prayer list to recall to his memory things he felt he should pray for. The question is not so much what posture we adopt, as it is the underlying reason for adopting it, and its effect on our prayer life. In this case, the Christian leader's purpose was to make his praying more effective.

As to kneeling when we pray, this is proper since we are addressing the God who made us, the One to whom we all shall give account of our lives. Yet the Bible describes different postures for prayer. At the dedication of the Temple at Jerusalem, Solomon knelt (I Kings 8:54), and in Ephesians 3:14 Paul speaks of bowing his knees in prayer. In administering the Old Testament rituals, the priests commonly stood. And we read of David, in II Samuel 7:18, that he went in "and sat before the LORD," to offer his prayer of thanksgiving to God. So one may stand, kneel, or sit while praying, and it can be acceptable to God. The question of posture in prayer, like the question of praying with eyes closed or open, is a matter of why we do what we do and what effect it has on our communion with God.

133. Should a Christian use a prayer book?

A criticism was made of a minister who wrote out his prayers and then read them at services, that he could not be said to pray from his heart. In all fairness I could not agree with this. Some persons do not "think on their feet," as we say, and become confused if they pray extemporaneously. They feel they are much more in the presence of God when they sit down by themselves, and go over their thoughts before God, and write them down. Such a person might be praying from the heart, and in faith, when he reads his prayer. The main thing is for a person to be sure he does pray from the heart, and by faith. A person might pray without premeditation and yet be repeating clichés, while exercising little faith or devotion.

Along a somewhat similar line, some persons use a prayer list as a reminder of those for whom they feel they should pray. Others think they should depend solely on the Holy Spirit to bring to their minds those for whom they should pray, believing that a prayer list is artificial and hence unspiritual. But prayer is not a memory contest, and I see no objection to a person's having a list, and consulting it, where necessary, if he desires to pray for certain persons, or about particular activities.

A prayer book is different, since it is composed by someone else, and ordinarily we would say that a person does better to pray simply from his own heart instead of using the words of another. Yet we must remember that some persons who are not well taught in Scripture, and who are deficient in their knowledge of English, might feel edified by reading the prayers of others, and in reading them, could very well unite their hearts with what they are reading. So while we do not recommend the reading of prayers from a book in contrast with praying freely from one's heart, yet we do not necessarily condemn those who do so, if the elements of faith and devotion are in their hearts in doing so, and provided the prayers are scriptural in content.

134. Does God answer a prayer such as Psalm 109?

In Acts 1:16 the Apostle Peter stated that the Holy Spirit spoke of Judas in the Old Testament "by the mouth of David." He presently quoted Psalm 69:25 and 109:8. This reminds us that while David was the human author of both these psalms, they were really the proclamation of the Holy Spirit. We believe it is wrong to attribute the desires expressed by David to purely human desire for revenge upon his personal enemies. They rather express God's judgment on His enemies. While Judas is not named in either psalm, Peter assured the disciples gathered together that Judas was in God's mind. No doubt God had in mind not only Judas but all the enemies of God and His truth.

One commentator calls attention to the fact that the enemies of God bring judgment not only upon themselves but often upon their families. Daniel's accusers and their families were cast into the den of lions. Drunkards often bring misery, and sometimes disease, upon members of their families as the result of the person's sins.

This commentator says: "The language accordingly of this psalm [the 109th] is judicial and prophetic. Enemies of Messiah and the Word of God will be judged (vv. 6-7); and the righteousness of their punishment and the grounds for it are set out in verses 8 to 20."

This commentator also states: "The passage, verses 8 to 15, is prophetic. It should be read in the future tense. . . . It predicts the sure consequences and fruit of hatred to the Word of God and to His people. . . . It is foolish to object to and argue against facts. There is a modern unhealthy sentiment against punishment. The prophetic prayers of the New Testament demanding judgment upon the opponents of the gospel are as terrible as those of the Old Testament foretelling, and approving, the destruction of the opponents of truth and grace." Among other illustrations of his point he refers to Christ's condemnation of the Pharisees in Matthew 23.

Some expositors, in an endeavor to soften what seems the harsh tone of this and similar psalms, have argued that these imprecations are to be understood as the taunts of the enemies of David and the children of God; but, as the *Wycliffe Commentary* states, this theory is not convincing. Several notice that the psalm may not be purely personal, but may refer to the enemies of the children of God from Abel down (Matt. 23:35). Verse 20 of the psalm seems to confirm this. The Apostle Paul wrote, in II Thessalonians 1:6, "It is a righteous thing with God to recompense tribulation to them that trouble you." See also Jude 15.

We must remember that while the psalm speaks of judgment in this world, those referred to are subjects of the eternal wrath of God.

135. If prayer is not answered at once, is it lack of faith to repeat the request? Could this be considered "vain repetition"?

The Bible teaches, both by example and precept, that it is not lack of faith to repeat a request made to God in prayer. In the Garden of Gethsemane the Lord Jesus repeated a request three times, and Matthew 26:44 and Mark 14:39 indicate that He said "the same words." The Apostle Paul also prayed three times concerning the "thorn in the flesh," which God sent him: "For this thing I besought the Lord thrice that it might depart from me" (II Cor. 12:8).

The teaching of Scripture is in accord with this. In Luke 11 the Lord Jesus gave the illustration of the man who had no food to set before a friend who arrived at his house near midnight. The man went to a neighbor's house to borrow bread. The neighbor was disinclined to give the man what he asked for, but he kept asking until his request was granted. God is not an unwilling giver, like the neighbor, but for various reasons may see fit to delay His answer to our prayer. If our request is in His will, it is right to repeat it.

Luke 18 teaches a similar lesson. There we read of a certain widow who pleaded her case before an unjust judge until he became wearied, and granted her request. God is not an unjust judge, but the application the Lord Jesus made was this: "And shall not God avenge his own elect, which cry day and night unto him, although he bear long with them? I tell you that he will avenge them speedily." For His own reasons God "bears long," yet when His time comes He will avenge speedily those who have been crying to Him "day and night."

The "vain repetition" which the Lord Jesus condemns in Matthew 6:7 is not the repetition of requests, even using the same words, as He Himself did in the Garden of Gethsemane. He condemns the idea that God will hear for "much speaking," i.e., multiplied words. This means endless repetition of formulated prayers. He does not criticize coming to God on many occasions with the same request which burdens one's heart. In some religions people engage in vain repetition of prayers by inscribing them on wooden drums, which are then turned by a water wheel. Another illustration of vain repetition is found in the prophecy of Isaiah, who accused the people of his generation of bowing down their heads like a bulrush (Isa. 58:5). Many people bow their heads when prayer is made, but without entering into it in spirit, and they are like a bulrush bowing down when the wind blows, and straightening up again when it stops. "Vain repetition" may also include prayers which are "said" or "recited," instead of being the earnest entreaty of the heart, presented to God in faith.

SALVATION

136. What is conversion? Is it really necessary?

In common usage, the word "conversion" often signifies a change from one religious group to another. In the Bible, the word is used in two ways. Sometimes it refers to the initial act of turning to Christ in faith for salvation. But another usage refers to restoration from a period or state of backsliding on the part of a child of God.

Matthew 18:3 illustrates the first of these two usages. There conversion is shown to be a necessity for salvation: "Verily I say unto you, Except ye be converted, and become as little children, ye shall not enter into the kingdom of heaven." In this use of the word man is viewed as having turned his back on God, as we read in Isaiah 53:6: "All we like sheep have gone astray; we have turned every one to his own way: and the LORD hath laid on him the iniquity of us all." In this usage the word conversion means turning back to God and coming to Him through faith in Christ, and has nothing to do, essentially, with affiliation with any particular religious group.

Psalm 19:7 illustrates the second usage of the word. "The law of the LORD is perfect, converting the soul." Taken by itself, this text could be understood either way, but the Hebrew word is the same word translated "restoreth" in Psalm 23:3 ("He restoreth my soul"). There the word seems clearly to refer to restoration and refreshing of the believer. It is in this sense that the Lord referred to conversion when He said to Peter, "When thou art converted, strengthen thy brethren" (Luke 22:32). Peter was already a "convert" in the sense of having openly acknowledged Jesus Christ as his Lord and Saviour.

144

137. Isn't it true that many people are born with Christian beliefs?

Children are born into an atmosphere of Christian belief by being born into a Christian family. This in no way guarantees that the child will grow up to be a Christian. Ephesians 2:3 states plainly that we "were by nature the children of wrath, even as others." The words, "I was shapen in iniquity, and in sin did my mother conceive me" (Ps. 51:5), make it clear that parents impart a sinful nature to their children. No sin is involved in the bearing of children, but we can only impart to them the nature which we ourselves possess—a fallen nature. Hence children naturally turn to the practice of sin. Psalm 58:3 says, "The wicked are estranged from the womb: they go astray as soon as they be born, speaking lies."

Divine life can only be imparted by the Holy Spirit. For this reason men "must be born again" (John 3:7). No one comes to Christ except by the conviction of the Holy Spirit. Jesus said, "No man can come to me, except the Father which hath sent me draw him" (John 6:44). This explains why often children of Christian parents (and especially of preachers) do not turn out well. Spiritual grace cannot be imparted by natural birth.

138. How can Christians say theirs is the only way to God?

If we believe in God, we must acknowledge that His will is absolute, and everyone must be subject to Him, whether voluntarily or involuntarily. The Bible claims to be the authoritative revelation of God to man, and it portrays Jesus Christ as His unique Son. If this claim were to be proved untrue, the Bible and the knowledge of God portrayed in the Bible would be invalidated. But if this claim be true, there can be no alternative to God's eternal truth and to His sovereignty in the affairs of mankind.

The matter resolves itself into whether the Bible is a true revelation of God, and whether Jesus Christ, as the Bible declares, is the only way of approach to God. If these claims are substantiated, they invalidate any other concept of God, and of man's relationship to Him.

139. Won't God forgive a person if he does the best he can?

The forgiveness of sins involves the character of God. God is holy, and He is the Judge of all the earth. Psalm 89:14 says, "Justice and judgment are the habitation of thy throne." The word *habitation* is otherwise translated "foundation." For God to forgive sins without dealing with them judicially would result in the overthrow of His throne—His righteous rule.

David forgave his son Absalom without dealing with Absalom's sin of murder. Unrepentant, Absalom soon plotted the murder of his father, and while his scheme was not successful, he did usurp David's throne for a time (II Sam. 14–18). This shows the necessity for a righteous ground for forgiveness.

Any work produced out of a sinful nature must fall short of the glory of God (Rom. 3:23). "So then they that are in the flesh cannot please God" (Rom. 8:8). Isaiah 64:6 says, "All our righteousnesses are as filthy rags." Thus no work of ours could ever make us acceptable to God. Sin, which separates us from God (Isa. 59:2), must be removed, and this can only be done through the blood of Christ's atonement (I John 1:7).

140. Won't God accept anyone, provided he is sincere?

Sincerity is commendable but not adequate to bring us into a right relationship to God. A person can be sincerely mistaken. One who takes carbolic acid believing it is cough medicine still suffers its effects. A person may sincerely believe a lie, but this does not change the lie to truth. A man who trusts himself to a bridge that is too weak to support him will find the bridge giving way, even though he has sincerely trusted in it. Weak faith in a strong bridge is more rewarding. A timid person can cross a strong bridge with safety.

The basis of approach to God is repentance and the obedience of faith (Acts 20:21). The essence of sin is rebellion against God, and repentance is the reversal of that attitude. In the obedience of faith we accept God's revelation of Himself to us in the person of His Son, and submit our lives to Him. True sincerity leads to this end.

We may add that it is only because of Christ's atonement that we can find acceptance with God. "Without shedding of blood there is no remission" (Heb. 9:22), and "the blood of Jesus Christ his [God's] Son cleanseth us from all sin" (I John 1:7).

141. If God wants everyone to be saved, why doesn't He speak miraculously so no one can miss the way?

This question assumes that all men are willing to be saved, which is not the case (Rom. 10:16). In the beginning, God in His sovereignty elected to create man with the power of choice. For God arbitrarily to insist that all men must receive His salvation would nullify His purpose in bringing man into existence.

God has purposely made the way of salvation simple and plain. The Lord Jesus said, "I am the way, the truth, and the life: no man cometh unto the Father but by me" (John 14:6). Our eternal salvation depends upon our attitude toward the Lord Jesus Christ. We can be sure that anyone desiring salvation, who comes to God in humility and faith, will accept God's provision, and be accepted of Him.

142. Can a person who is once truly saved ever be lost again?

In John 10:27-30 we read, "My sheep hear my voice, and I know them, and they follow me: and I give unto them eternal life; and they shall never perish, neither shall any man pluck them out of my hand. My Father, which gave them me, is greater than all, and no man [literally, no one] is able to pluck them out of my Father's hand. I and my Father are one." This is a flat assertion that no sheep of Christ shall ever perish, and this is confirmed by the rest of the New Testament teaching on this subject.

When a person trusts in Christ his sins are forgiven, and he is born again in the power of the Holy Spirit. He *has* everlasting life (John 3:36), and these things are all stated as a present experience. Acts 13:38-39 states that believers in Christ *are* justified. Hebrews 10:17 says, "Their sins and iniquities will I remember no more." Psalm 103:12 says our sins are removed from us "as far as the east is from the west." They are cast "into the depths of the sea" (Micah 7:19), behind God's back (Isaiah 38:17). We also lose our status as being "in Adam," and are now "alive to God *in Christ Jesus*" (Rom. 6:11, where the word *through* is literally "in"). Ephesians 2:6 says God "hath raised us up together, and made us sit together in heavenly places in Christ Jesus."

For a Christian to become lost after being truly saved would require the reversal of all this. God would have to deny His Word, and remember what He promised to forget; our sins would have to be brought up from the depths of the sea and charged to us again. We would have to be taken out of Christ and put back into Adam; and all of this (and other things as well) would mean we had done something which the blood of Christ didn't cover, for if we really trusted in His blood, that should have atoned for all our sins.

It is never stated in Scripture that Christ put away *some* of our sins. The very nature of the atonement requires that His death put away *all* sins, or none at all. "The wages of sin is death," and Christ either paid the penalty, or He didn't. Before He died He cried with a loud voice, "It is finished." The warning that He shall say to some, "I never knew you," refers to a false profession of one who never came in true repentance and faith. He does not say, "I knew you once, but not now," but rather, "I *never* knew you." They had not been saved at all.

143. Does Hebrews 6:4-6 teach that a person can be saved and later lost again?

No, I do not believe *any* Scripture teaches this, although there are those who consider this passage a proof text for that view.

Otherwise two views are commonly held about this text. (1) It describes believers who become unfaithful to the Lord and who lose permanently their privilege of serving Him. (2) It describes people who went along with Christianity, embracing it without actually experiencing the new birth; and who then forsook all profession of faith in Christ.

Various elements enter into this difference of view. We have already explained that we do not believe anyone becomes saved, and later is lost. Those who view the passage as speaking of true believers consider that what is said could not apply to one who was not saved. On the other hand, some of us believe that what is said in condemnation could not apply to a true believer and that it does not describe dismissal from service but being lost forever. This is true of apostates.

Looking at the passage in this way we take it that such persons as Balaam and Judas were enlightened. Balaam gave four discourses which show considerable breadth of knowledge of God's mind (Numbers 23 and 24), and Scripture indicates that the Spirit of God empowered him to do so. In the case of Judas, there seems to be no reason to doubt that he cast out demons by the power of the Spirit of God. Perhaps the Lord's words in Luke 10:20 were a hint to Judas to make sure he became truly saved: "In this rejoice not, that the spirits are subject unto you; but rather rejoice because your names are written in heaven."

When people were becoming saved by thousands, as at the time of Pentecost, no doubt many who came under the power of the gospel were like those described in the parable of the sower—those represented by the seed which fell on stony ground, where there was not much earth. The seed did not take root, although it sprang up out of the seed itself, and when the sun shone upon it, it withered. This description could well apply to the experience of the people referred to in Hebrews 6.

The expression "have tasted of the good word of God" can mean either to taste in the sense of appropriating or to taste without appropriating. One's interpretation will depend on one's view of the passage as a whole. In my thinking, they tasted without appropriating. Hence, under pressure, they fell away. It is not said that they fell into sin. The word translated "fall away" occurs only here in the New Testament. They evidently went back to Judaism and its ritual, not as being ignorant of the gospel, but as understanding it, and rejecting it. They thus "crucified to *themselves* the Son of God" (v. 6), taking their stand with those who had done so. The word "afresh" is not in the best attested text.

The illustration given in verses 7-8 shows that these people had the same opportunity of grace as others but did not profit by it. The statement in verse 8 ("We are persuaded better things of you, and things that accompany salvation") seems to me to indicate that the writer is distinguishing those who remained faithful from those who were not saved at all.

144. If a person once saved cannot be lost, what is the meaning of the words, "He that endureth to the end shall be saved"? Also, how does this apply in the case of the servant who said, "My lord delayeth his coming," and began to beat his fellow-servants?

The first quotation appears in Matthew 10:22; and the same thought appears in Matthew 24:13 and the passage parallel to the latter, Mark 13:13. In each case the words are in a context relating to the future time of judgment prophesied, which is called the Great Tribulation. It is that period to which Revelation 13 applies, in which we are told that unless a person receives the "mark of the beast" he will not be permitted to buy or sell; also that many will be put to death for refusing to worship the beast and his image.

But in Revelation 14:9-12 we are told that those who do receive the mark of the beast will be cast into the lake of fire and "shall drink of the wine of the wrath of God." Hence it will be of the utmost importance, during the Great Tribulation, to "endure to the end." That is to say, it will be of the utmost importance to refuse to worship this personage or to receive his mark, and to resist him either unto death or until the Lord comes and ends the beast's control of things.

If we consider the words "He that endureth to the end" out of context, we can say that true Christians *shall* endure in accordance with what we read in Romans 14:4, "he shall be holden up, for God is able to make him stand." In the case of the unfaithful steward, since we are told in Matthew 24:51 that his lord shall "appoint him his portion with the hypocrites," I take it that he was not a saved man to begin with, else he would not be a hypocrite.

145. Must I accept teachings like atonement, sin, and hell?

Acceptance of these doctrines is basic to an understanding of man's relationship to God. The subtleties and refinements of philosophy and psychology can never erase the guilt of sin or the accountability of man to God as his judge. We can explain sin; we can excuse it or rationalize concerning it; but this in no way alters the dictum of God that "the soul that sinneth it shall die."

Scripture is equally clear that "without shedding of blood is no remission" (Heb. 9:22). This statement has significance deeper than appears on the surface. "The wages of sin is death," and it is only as the penalty of sin is paid that God has a righteous ground on which to forgive sin. For God to forgive sin apart from atonement would be to violate the moral nature of God, and would affect His government of the universe. Violation of His laws would introduce a chaotic state from which we are spared because God has the characteristics described in the Bible.

To refuse to accept the doctrines of "atonement," "sin," and "hell," is like a criminal refusing to accept the penalties of the laws of the land. He may reject the laws, but he suffers the penalty just the same.

146. Should I become a Christian if I feel I can't live the life?

Christians are not expected to live the Christian life in their own strength. No one could do this. Part of the experience of conversion to Christ is being born again by the power of the

Holy Spirit (John 1:12-13). Also, the Bible teaches that the Holy Spirit comes to dwell within each believer (Eph. 1:13; Rom. 8:9). The indwelling Spirit gives believers the power to live for God.

This power is renewed day by day as we read God's Word and seek His help in prayer. "In the day when I cried thou answeredst me, and strengthenedst me with strength in my soul" (Ps. 138:3). In Ephesians 3:16 Paul prayed that believers might be "strengthened with might by his Spirit in the inner man." Without such support we would be sure to fail, but the Apostle Peter tells us that God has "given unto us all things that pertain unto life and godliness" (II Pet. 1:3).

147. I'd like to be a Christian, but I have tried and failed. What can I do?

Christianity is not "trying" but "trusting." We are saved not by what we do for God but by what God has done for us in giving His Son to be our Saviour. Christ's work of atonement is a finished, perfect work, as He declared when He hung on the cross (John 19:30). Salvation is "by grace . . . through faith" (Eph. 2:8). "By grace" means it is free. "Through faith" means that we receive it as we submit ourselves to Christ and acknowledge Him as our Lord and Saviour (Rom. 10:9-10).

Good works are not acceptable to God as a means of obtaining salvation (Eph. 2:9).

Anything we do for God which is acceptable to Him must be the *fruit* of salvation (Eph. 2:10); "for it is God which worketh in you both to will and to do of his good pleasure" (Phil. 2:13). A person who has been rescued from drowning does not show his gratitude to the one who saved him in order to become saved, but because he is now safe.

The work of saving sinners is Christ's. (See Matthew 1:21: "Thou shalt call his name JESUS: for he shall save his people from their sins.") We cannot share in the work of salvation, but it is required of us that we show by our lives that we have truly trusted Christ. Our works are not the *basis* of our salvation, but the *evidence* that we have trusted in Him.

148. Why should I become a Christian when some Christians do things I wouldn't do?

Our relationship to God should never be governed by the failures of others. Romans 14:12 says: "So then every one of us shall give account of himself to God." While Christ died for the world, He also died for us individually, and each of us is responsible to receive Him by faith as our Saviour and to submit our life to Him. The failures of others will not constitute an acceptable excuse for our failure to obey the will of God in our own life.

149. How can a person be sure he is saved, since the Bible speaks of some who thought they were saved and later found out they were not?

There are two bases of assurance—the Word of God and the Spirit of God. Basic to my relationship to God is my acceptance of what He says in the Bible about me, and about His Son, and what His Son has done for me. We learn from the Bible that God has promised that on the ground of repentance and faith He will forgive the sins of all who come to Him through Christ. Peter spoke of this to the household of Cornelius (Acts 10:43), and Paul preached the same message in the synagogue at Antioch of Pisidia (Acts 13:38-41).

In salvation there is a sequence of fact, faith, and feeling. Many persons rely on their feelings for assurance, but feelings are changeable and therefore unreliable. We must rely on certain facts revealed in God's Word, and accept the facts by faith. God says, "All have sinned" (Rom. 3:23). In Acts 17:30-31 Paul preached that God now commands "all men every where to repent." This means to turn away from sin to Christ, in faith. Then comes the promise of salvation to whosoever believeth. We can rest on these because they are in the unchanging Word of God.

If by faith I have submitted myself to Christ, acknowledging my sins and desiring His salvation, His Word assures me that I have everlasting life (John 3:36 and others). I can rest with assurance on His Word. The Holy Spirit is given to all believers (Eph. 1:13-14), and His working in a believer will produce the Christian feelings and exercises which will confirm his assurance that he is saved (I John 3:24).

150. Are believers in non-Christian religions lost?

The basic question is not one of "religion" but of one's relationship to God. The Bible teaches that all humanity is involved in sin and is, therefore, under the judgment of God. We are spiritually "dead in trespasses and sins" (Eph. 2:1). The Apostle Peter told the Jewish Sanhedrin, "Neither is there salvation in any other: for there is none other name under heaven given among men, whereby we must be saved" (Acts 4:12). The "name" is identified in verse 10: "Jesus Christ of Nazareth, whom ye crucified, whom God raised from the dead." It was in this name that the miracle of healing had been performed which was the cause of the strife at that time.

To say that man may adopt any form of religion and find acceptance with God would be a denial of these truths. Sincere belief in a false god, or in false teaching, does not provide a valid way of approach to God. A person can take poison, sincerely believing it to be medicine, but his sincerity will not deliver him from its harmful effects.

It was the rejection of the knowledge of the true God (Rom. 1:20-28) which led to the worship of false gods and gave rise to the development of false religions. They are not to be believed in, but to be repented of. Paul and Barnabas said to the idolaters at Lystra, "We . . . preach unto you that ye should turn from these vanities unto the living God" (Acts 14:15).

151. Does John 2 teach that Jesus can be approached only through Mary, His mother?

Mary was highly honored among women by being chosen of God to be the mother of Christ. We do not believe that this deifies her, or that it gives her permanent influence over the Lord Jesus. We read that in His boyhood He was subject to Joseph and Mary (Luke 2:51), but in His manhood, and especially in His public ministry, He did always and only the will of His Father in heaven.

The incident in John 2 was at a marriage at Cana of Galilee. When they ran out of wine, Mary relayed this fact to Jesus. His reply was, "Woman, what have I to do with thee? mine hour is not yet come." It is literally, "What to me and to thee?" However, Mary, anticipating some action on His part, instructed the servants to do whatever Jesus commanded them. The Lord then performed His first miracle by turning the water into wine.

That He did not do this merely because of her request is seen by a comparison of this passage with John 7, where we read how His brothers urged Him to go to Jerusalem. He responded by telling them, "Go ye up unto this feast: I go not yet unto this feast; for mine hour is not yet come" (v. 8). Yet soon after they went, He went also, obviously not because of their urging but because it was His Father's will. The same was true at the wedding feast in Cana (John 2).

When Mary and the Lord's brothers sought Him, as recorded in Mark 3:33-35, He said, "Who is my mother, or my brethren? And he looked round about on them which sat about him, and said, Behold my mother and my brethren! For whosoever shall do the will of God, the same is my brother, and my sister, and mother." Later, when someone said, "Blessed is the womb that bare thee, and the paps which thou hast sucked," He replied, "Yea rather, blessed are they that hear the word of God, and keep it." (See Luke 11:27-28.)

There is no suggestion that Jesus in His manhood and in His public ministry was influenced in any special way by His mother. Acts 1:12-14 indicates that Mary joined the disciples in praying to Jesus, but again there is no suggestion that she had any priority over them in such supplication.

152. Why ask me to accept your religion? I have one of my own.

The most important thing in the life of any person is the salvation of his soul. In Mark 8:36 the Lord Jesus asked, "What shall it profit a man, if he shall gain the whole world, and lose his own soul?" The Lord also declared, "No man cometh unto the Father, but by me" (John 14:6). If His claim to be the Son of God in the unique sense of being part of the Holy Trinity is valid, then any other form of approach to God is ruled out. Jesus declared emphatically, "Except a man be born again, he cannot see the kingdom of God" (John 3:3).

A person who has religion and does not have vital faith in Christ is under a delusion which, if not corrected, will prove eternally disastrous. If you are out of Christ, the person who disturbs your complacency is doing you the greatest possible favor. Since men do not, by nature, seek after God (Rom. 3:11), Christians are responsible to share with others their knowledge of God's salvation. A person who is led to know Christ as Saviour will be forever grateful to anyone who awakens him to his need of Christ.

153. If, when we are born again, our sins are remembered no more (Hebrews 10:17), and removed from us "as far as the east is from the west" (Psalm 103:12), why is it said, "So then every one of us shall give account of himself to God" (Romans 14:12)?

The statements regarding the forgiveness and removal of sin have to do with our relationship to God as the One who is Judge of all the earth (Gen. 18:25). God dealt with sin judicially at the cross, when He laid our sins on His Son, who put them away by the sacrifice of Himself (Heb. 9:26). Because Christ paid the penalty of our sins in full by His death and resurrection and the shedding of His blood, God can now offer pardon to all who trust in Him. As one hymn-writer puts it, this forgiveness is "full and free." It is full because it covers every sin. It is free because the penalty is completely paid.

This latter fact is often misunderstood, because many persons think the penalty of sin is suffering. While suffering is included, the basic penalty of sin is *death*. This death is not merely physical; it includes eternal separation from God. Consequently, salvation must be the gift of God to us. It is impossible to obtain salvation in any other way.

Christ could purchase salvation for us only because of who He is. Were He not the infinite Son of God, His death could not have sufficed to make atonement for the sins of the world. The deity of Christ is basic to Christianity, as is also His incarnation, His atoning death, and His resurrection.

It remains true, however, that the life of each of us shall come into review before God. For unbelievers, this will be at the Great White Throne (Rev. 20:11 ff.). Such persons will be there because they have not believed on God's Son (John 3:36), and the measure of their judgment will be "according to their works" (Rev. 20:12). A number of scriptures show that there will be differing degrees of severity in the judgment of God.

The believer will never come before the Great White Throne, because his sins were dealt with in the Person of God's Son. But he will appear before the judgment seat of Christ (II Cor. 5:10) where the believer's works will be examined, and rewards will be given commensurate with our Lord's estimate of their value (I Cor. 3:10–4:5). Christ's estimate will be based not only on what we have done but on why and how we have done these things. Since the effectiveness of our works depends partly on the purity and depth of our spiritual life, all of this will come into review. This is not a contradiction of the fact that all our sin and failure was judicially forgiven at the cross. The judgment of believers at the judgment seat of Christ will be for a different purpose, and no question of divine and eternal penalty will be raised.

A believer must give still another accounting for his sins. This

has to do with our daily communion with God. Sin, forgiven
judicially because of the atoning death of Christ, is nevertheless
defiling to the believer; and while it does not break his relationship to God as His child, it does mar his fellowship with God as
his Father. This is the forgiveness described in I John 1:9.
Judicial forgiveness is, of necessity, a once-for-all experience, in
which *all* sin is put away. Under God's laws, which are absolute
and demand the penalty of death for a single sin (James 2:10),
a sinner cannot be partly forgiven. Judicial forgiveness cannot
be piecemeal.

On the other hand, in the matter of the believer's daily fellowship with God, sins must be dealt with specifically and separately.
The consciousness of sin hinders our freedom in approaching God
in prayer, and toleration of known sin in our lives grieves and
quenches the Holy Spirit within us. But by confessing of our
sin and forsaking it by His grace, and in His power, fellowship
is restored, and the power of God can operate in our lives.

**154. At what age should a child be baptized and taken into the
church, in a church which believes in adult baptism, and
which requires conversion to Christ as a prerequisite for
church membership?**

By "adult baptism" we do not mean, of course, baptism on the
basis of age, but on the basis of what is considered a responsible
confession of Christ as Saviour. In a previous question I discussed
the possibility of a young child being saved (see question 129).
Where there is doubt, I think that if the child's profession seems
sincere, and the parents and Sunday school teacher believe it to
be so, the pastor might take this into consideration with regard
to both baptism and church membership.

Some parents are overoptimistic about their children, while
others are ultraconservative. If those who know the children best
have reason to believe they are genuinely converted to Christ,
their profession can be accepted at face value. Even with adults
a seemingly promising profession sometimes turns out to be a
false one, as in the case of Simon Magus (Acts 8). When such a

condition becomes manifest, it should be dealt with accordingly. Normally, when a person has true faith in Christ, his life and habits and associations give evidence of such faith.

155. Does the story of the "rich young ruler" teach salvation by works?

This story is found in Matthew 19, in Luke 18, and in Mark 10. It tells of a young man who was rich and a ruler, who ran to Christ and kneeled before Him, asking, "Good Master, what shall I do to inherit eternal life?" The Lord's answer has mystified many persons, and from more than one angle.

Many think that the Lord, when He asked the young man why he called Him "good," was disclaiming deity. The Lord's question was intended rather to evoke from him a statement of how he viewed Christ. Since the ruler in his second reply did not use the word "good," we may presume that he did not acknowledge the deity of Christ.

Also, some versions indicate that the Lord's question was two-fold. The first part of the question ("Why askest thou me concerning that which is good?") might be rephrased this way: "Are you addressing me as Deity?" and the second, "Do you think you can meet the requirements for being good?" The young man's answer to the first was "No," and to the second his answer was "Yes," since he claimed to have kept the commandments from his youth up.

Since his answer to both questions was based on false premises, he was not ready to be saved, and the Lord gave him what amounted to a test of the genuineness of his claim to have kept the law, which involved loving his neighbor as himself. He soon proved his inability to keep the law in its true meaning, for "he went away sorrowful," giving no indication that he meant to do what the Lord instructed him to do. We should not infer from Jesus' conversation with this young man that keeping the law would give a person eternal life. Leviticus 18:5 indicates that a person who truly kept the law would not be subject to the penalty of death in physical life. But no one does perfectly keep the law. This is what the young ruler should have learned from this conversation with the Lord Jesus. Salvation and eternal life are gained only by faith in Christ, and on the ground of His atonement.

156. Do rituals of different faiths make a difference in being a Christian?

In the matter of *becoming* a Christian, ritual plays no part whatever. We are saved not by any ritualistic procedure but by the exercise of faith in our hearts. Wherever we read the gospel message in the New Testament, salvation is declared to be "by grace, through faith" (Eph. 2:8-9). This means salvation is free, but God cannot give it to us apart from our acceptance of Christ by faith.

Salvation's being free is not because it is cheap; to provide it God had to give His Son to die for our sins. It is free because it is paid for by the precious blood—the atoning blood—of Christ. Hence there is nothing for us to do to *merit* salvation; that would be impossible for us. We receive it as a gift, but on the condition of faith, which implies repentance for sin and a willingness to submit our lives to Christ in the obedience of faith (Rom. 16:26).

Ritualistic observances, insofar as they have validity at all, give expression to our faith. In such matters we must be guided by the instructions of Scripture. Some rituals are manifestly without any scriptural foundation, but may not be in *violation* of any teaching of Scripture. We ought to avoid anything which is contrary to the Word of God.

157. If salvation is left to man's choice, does not this make him, in a sense, his own saviour?

It can rightly be said that salvation is all of God. The desire for it originated with Him, and not with man. We read in Romans 3:11, "There is none that seeketh after God." The plan for salvation (involving Christ's atonement) was devised by God

and executed by God, through His Son. Salvation is not by any
work of man. Even given the plan, man could never have brought
it into effect. Further, salvation is offered to man on the initiative
of God, and is witnessed to by those who have already received
it in faith. Salvation is made effective in us by the regenerating
power of the Holy Spirit. Salvation is all of God, and all of grace.

Yet God has given man his choice, either to receive Christ in
repentance and faith, or to reject Him. Unless one submits to
Christ, under the conviction of the Holy Spirit, God will not
arbitrarily save him, for God in His sovereignty has not only
provided salvation but He has also set the terms on which it is
given to man. Ephesians 2:8-9 says, "For by grace are ye saved
through faith; and that not of yourselves: it is the gift of God:
not of works, lest any man should boast."

Some have the idea that even the taking of salvation by faith
as a gift could be considered an act of merit on man's part. But
Romans 3:27 says: "Where is boasting then? It is excluded. By
what law? of works? Nay: but by the law of faith." Calvin's
comment is: "Not even as a reward justly due to faith, but because we receive by faith what God freely gives." Man has not
only the power to make a choice, but he is confronted with the
necessity to do so. "No choice" is considered a choice against
Christ, as He Himself said in Matthew 12:30. Pilate washed his
hands and declared his innocence, yet he is listed, in Acts 4:27,
with the enemies of Christ.

158. If a believer dies with unconfessed sin, what will God do with him, especially if he has just committed a sin?

A person's status with God does not depend on the last act of
his life, but on his relationship to the Lord Jesus Christ. If a
person has trusted in Christ, and has acknowledged Him as his
Lord and Saviour, that person is born of God, and has the right
to be called a child of God (John 1:12-13). God, as the Judge
of all the earth, dealt with the believer's sins at the cross. Of
necessity this was done on a "once-for-all" basis, and gives the
believer acceptance with God through Christ.

The grace of God that saves us also teaches us "that, denying ungodliness and worldly lusts, we should live soberly, righteously, and godly [piously] in this present world" (Titus 2:12). The sins of a believer mar his communion with God, though not his relationship as God's child, which is based on Christ's atonement and the regenerating work of the Holy Spirit. But even sinful thoughts grieve the Holy Spirit and quench His working in the children of God. Cleansing and restoration depend on our confessing and forsaking any known sin (Proverbs 28:13; I John 1:9—2:2).

But there is a difference between God dealing with us as Judge, and dealing with us as Father. If He has to deal with us as Judge, it is because we are before Him in our sins, and the penalty is eternal judgment. But if we have confessed our lost condition and have come to God through Christ's atonement, we will never come into *that* judgment. Sin is no longer our master, and we its slave, because of the atonement of Christ and the indwelling Holy Spirit. Any sins we may commit are still heinous to God, but He deals with us as His children and not as prisoners at the bar.

A person who is a believer and falls into some sin does not thereby cease to be a child of God. This would mean that the value of Christ's atonement is nullified by an act of sin on our part. The very purpose of Christ's atonement was to pay the penalty of our sin. If a sin on the part of a believer could nullify the value of the atonement, then what did the atonement accomplish? If a sin does not nullify the atonement, then the believer's relationship to God is secure. However, if he dies with unconfessed sin in his life it will be to his shame. But he does not lose his salvation because the sin came at the end of his life.

159. How can you separate salvation and divine healing as God's will for all His children?

I do not question God's power to heal, with or without medicine, nor do I question His power to sustain His children in any trial He permits to come to them. But I do not believe it is necessarily God's will that His children should always be in good health. We find in the Bible that some were sick without their illness being attributed to their being out of the will of God. Paul wrote to Timothy about his "often infirmity," but does not suggest it was due to anything wrong in Timothy's state of soul. In fact, Timothy is the only person in the New Testament who is called "a man of God." This does not mean he was the only one who had that character, but he is the only one so described.

Other cases of sickness are alluded to in the New Testament, as when Paul wrote, in II Timothy 4:20, "Trophimus have I left at Miletum sick." John, in his third epistle, said, "The elder unto the well-beloved Gaius, whom I love in the truth. Beloved, I wish above all things that thou mayest prosper and be in health, even as thy soul prospereth." It seems that while Gaius was in a good state of soul, his health and prosperity were not commensurate with his piety. Often in the history of the church persons who have been sick or invalid most of their lives have given us the choicest writings and Christian poetry, showing they have experienced largely the mercies of God, and His comforts.

But we are not left to example. Romans 8:19-25 plainly tells us, "The whole creation groaneth and travaileth in pain together until now. And not only they, but ourselves also, which have the firstfruits of the Spirit, even we ourselves groan within ourselves, waiting for the adoption, to wit, the redemption of our body. For we are saved by hope: but hope that is seen is not hope; for what a man seeth, why doth he yet hope for it? But if we hope for that we see not, then do we with patience wait for it." When Christ's redemption is applied to our bodies, it will not be a matter of patching up these old ones, but their being glorified "like unto his glorious body" (Phil. 3:21). Meantime we experience the providential goodness of God as our Father in all matters relating to this life, whether of health or prosperity. (See Matthew 6.)

160. How can a believer be saved (I Corinthians 3:15) if all his works are burned up?

The context in which the verse referred to appears (I Cor. 3:10-15) distinguishes between salvation and rewards. Salvation is based on what Christ did for us in His sufferings and death and the shedding of His blood. He bore the penalty of our sins, and delivers all who trust in Him from this judgment. Until a person is saved, he cannot do anything for God which will be accepted by Him. (See Romans 8:8, "So then they that are in the flesh cannot please God.") But Ephesians 2:10 shows that God has designed that those who are saved should serve Him, and that He has a plan for their lives.

I Corinthians 3:10-15 is speaking of this, our building on Christ, the true and only foundation for the Church and for the life of the believer. But we are warned that each person's work is going to be tested as by fire. That which is done according to God's Word and in the power of the Holy Spirit will (like the gold, silver, and precious stones) abide this test, and result in reward. But works done in contravention of God's Word and in the energy of the flesh will be like the wood, hay, and stubble. Such works shall be burned up, and the believer will suffer loss; but the person's salvation will not be brought into question. However, some think that this passage presents a hypothetical case and that no true believer will have *all* his works burned up. But the fact of this judgment and the nature of it are described here.

161. If faith is the gift of God, as Ephesians 2:8 seems to indicate, does this mean that only those can be saved to whom this gift is given?

It has often been pointed out that the Greek word for "faith" in Ephesians 2:8 is feminine, while the pronoun is neuter, indicating that it is not faith which is declared to be "the gift of God." This becomes clearer when we translate the pronoun as "this," instead of "that." The text then reads: "For by grace are ye saved through faith; and this not of yourselves; it is the gift of God."

The salvation is not of yourselves, it is the gift of God. Man's power of choice makes him responsible to receive Christ by faith as his Saviour, but such receiving of Christ does not give him any meritorious part in procuring that salvation.

162. Don't you agree God will save a man in His own time?

There is a sense in which we cannot approach God without action on His part. "No man can come to me, except the Father which hath sent me draw him" (John 6:44). However, I believe that God uses all kinds of incidents and circumstances to speak to people, and it would be wrong for an individual to wait for some special or striking revelation of God.

In view of the uncertainty of life, it is well to keep in mind the words of II Corinthians 6:2, "Behold, now is the accepted time; behold, now is the day of salvation." This implies that whenever a person is made conscious, by any means, of his need of salvation, it is God's time for him to come to Him through faith in Christ. A person can have no assurance that he will have another opportunity to do so.

SIN AND EVIL

163. The Bible says God creates evil (Isaiah 45:7), and that He makes the wrath of man to praise Him (Psalm 76:10). Does this mean that evil originates with God?

No, it does not. God is a holy God, and it is wrong to think He would bring evil into existence. If He did, He could hardly judge those who practice it. Evil is abhorrent to Him. In James 1:13 we read that "God cannot be tempted with evil, neither tempteth he any man." The writer of Psalm 76 said, in verse 10, "Surely the wrath of man shall praise thee: the remainder of wrath shalt thou restrain," but this does not mean that God condones any evil committed by anyone. He overrules men's rebellious and sinful acts to bring about His purposes in spite of them. He could not be the author of rebellion against Himself.

God said, in Isaiah 45:7, "I form the light, and create darkness: I make peace, and create evil. I the LORD do all these things." The "evil" here is in contrast with "peace," not "righteousness." It has the sense of "adversity." If we take Ezekiel 28:11-17 as an enigmatic description of Satan, the passage indicates that evil originated with him. And if we take Isaiah 14:12-16 also to describe Satan, we get some idea of how this came about. There is no conflict in the fact that Ezekiel referred to the king of Tyre, and Isaiah to the king of Babylon, since Satan is the prince of this world, and is the spiritual head of its highest existing powers, apart from God.

Sin came into being because God gave to angels, and later to men, the power of choice. In the exercise of that choice, Satan, not satisfied with the place God gave him, decided to elevate himself. Apparently a large number of angels joined in this re-

166

bellion against God. Later, Satan persuaded Eve and, through
her, Adam, to seek a greater portion than God had assigned to
them as His creatures. This should speak to us, since much of
the frustration experienced by people of our day stems from their
not accepting the providences of God with regard to their limitations.

164. What is sin?

Sin has many aspects. A word commonly used for it in the
New Testament is found in Romans 3:23, where we read, "All
have sinned and come short of the glory of God." The Greek word
for "sinned" means to "miss a mark," and Vincent gives two illustrations: a warrior who throws a spear and fails to strike an adversary; or a traveler who misses his way. Anything short of perfection is sin.

Exodus 34:7 uses three words for sin: *iniquity, transgression,*
and *sin.* These suggest perversity; a violation of what is right,
or the rights of another; and failure to fulfill one's responsibility.

I John 3:4 says, "Sin is transgression of the law," though a better translation is "sin is lawlessness." This suggests a spirit of rebellion against the perfect will of God.

These are some of the basic concepts of sin, and sin began,
many believe, when Satan declared his five "I will's" (Isa. 14:13-
14) in opposition to God's will. When we are not subject to
God's control, we are open to the perversion of human desire, so
that various forms of immorality result, such as lying, stealing,
adultery, murder, and so on. These are the fruits and expression
of basic sin.

Not only are there sins of commission but also of omission. To
do something which we believe is wrong is a violation of conscience, and therefore wrong for us (Rom. 14:23, "Whatsoever
is not of faith is sin"). On the other hand, to fail to do what we
know is our duty to do is also sin (James 4:17, "To him that
knoweth to do good, and doeth it not, to him it is sin"). We see,
in Luke 7, that Simon the Pharisee prided himself on the fact
that he was not guilty of the kind of sin committed by the woman

who anointed the feet of Jesus. The Lord Jesus showed Simon he was guilty of sins of omission which indicated a heart far from God.

Sin is any fault or failure.

165. Is it true that the "original sin" was sexual relationship and that babies are baptized to cleanse them from this original sin?

Though widespread in some areas, the idea that the original sin of Adam and Eve was sexual intercourse is erroneous. They were commanded by God to "be fruitful, and multiply, and replenish [fill] the earth, and subdue it" (Gen. 1:28). God gave Eve to Adam to be his wife, so the marital relationship could not have been sinful. It gives a very wrong idea of life to consider it to be so, although sexual intercourse is often practiced in circumstances which *are* sinful.

Original sin was disobedience to God's command, eating the fruit of a tree which was forbidden by God. Since this was done before Adam and Eve had any children, the entire human race is viewed as having shared in that sin (Rom. 5:12). We therefore share in the effects of that sin; we are born with a sinful nature (Eph. 2:3) and are subject to the law of sin and death. We cannot be cleansed or delivered from sin by baptism but only by the atoning blood of Christ (Heb. 9:22).

Romans 5:15-21 shows that just as all human beings inherit the sinful state of Adam, so all believers in Christ share in the fruits of His atonement, including the forgiveness of sins, and the gift of eternal life. Many texts in the New Testament show that it is faith in Christ which brings us into possession of this salvation, e.g., John 1:12-13; 5:24; 3:36.

Baptism is viewed differently by various denominations. In the Bible, John's baptism is connected with the confession of sin and the desire for forgiveness; Christian baptism is connected with the acknowledgment of our faith in Christ, and expresses our identification with the persons of the Holy Trinity, as children of God. We do not believe that the physical act of baptism can cleanse the soul in the sight of God. See I Peter 3:21: "not the putting away of the filth of the flesh," and compare the similar principle in Micah 6:7. The death of Christ provides redemption not only from original sin but from all sin (I Pet. 2:24; I John 1:7).

166. Does the Bible speak of "greater" and "lesser'" sins? If so, what are they?

A letter accompanying the above question objected. to such a distinction being made. Yet we read in John 19:11 that the Lord Jesus said to Pilate, "He that delivered me unto thee hath the greater sin."

We must distinguish between the *fact* of sin, and the seriousness of the sin committed. The least violation of the will of God is just as definitely sin as the greatest. James 2:10 says: "Whosoever shall keep the whole law, and yet offend in one point, he is guilty of all." He who breaks God's law in one point is a lawbreaker, and is subject to God's judgment. But there are differing degrees of guilt and differing degrees of judgment.

We delude ourselves when we claim to be righteous because we are less sinful than others. One sin makes a man a sinner in God's sight. In Matthew 23:13-14 we read, "Woe unto you, scribes and Pharisees, hypocrites! for ye shut up the kingdom of heaven against men: . . . therefore ye shall receive the greater damnation [or, judgment]." Since there are differing degrees of judgment, there are evidently differing degrees of sin, but this does not imply that men should weigh one sin against another to see if one is worse than another.

Luke 12:47-48 teaches that the seriousness of sin is based partly on the degree of light and understanding which we must disregard in order to sin. The reference in Matthew 23 suggests that the seriousness of sin is also partly measured by its adverse effect on others. So there are degrees of guilt in connection with sin, and there are corresponding degrees in the judgment of God, as Revelation 20:11-15 shows.

In Matthew 11 we see how the Lord Jesus, in His condemnation of the cities of His day where His mighty works were done, confirmed the fact that greater privilege entails greater responsibility. The Bible never makes light of sin, yet even the law of Moses distinguished between such sins as murder and that of stealing; and punishment differed accordingly.

167. If sin is forgiven for the believer in Christ, why must a believer sometimes suffer the fruits of what he has done?

All who believe in Christ receive at once (at the time they receive Him as Saviour) the forgiveness of sins (Acts 10:43; 13:38-39) and eternal life (John 3:16, 36). They are born again (John 1:12-13). But we who are believers are left in this world which is suffering the effects of sin, and we continue to share the groaning of creation (Rom. 8:19-25). We do not become immune to the adverse effects of sin. If there is an epidemic, Christians become sick as readily as anyone else. In times of financial depression, Christians lose employment and money as quickly as anyone else. If there is drought, or famine, or whirlwind, Christians suffer with the rest.

By the same token, if a Christian has committed an offense against the laws of the land, or against another person, this offense is not cancelled by the fact that he has now become saved. He must still face the consequences of what he has done. And if, in his life before conversion to Christ, he lived in a way which damaged his body, often the consequences of these acts remain after conversion. Of course, the changed life will help to overcome some of these things, and no doubt God sometimes grants recovery from some of the effects of sin. But we cannot expect the complete removal of the effects of sin until the Lord comes. Then, as we read in I John 3:1-3, "We shall be like him, for we shall see him as he is." Then we shall be completely delivered from the presence of sin and all its adverse effects.

168. What is the unpardonable sin mentioned in Matthew 12:32?

This verse says: "Whosoever speaketh a word against the Son of man, it shall be forgiven him: but whosoever speaketh against the Holy Ghost, it shall not be forgiven him, neither in this world, neither in the world to come." Verse 31 makes it clear that the speaking "against" the Holy Spirit is "blasphemy"; that is, to speak maliciously or slanderously against a person. In this context, the speaking was not only impious and irreverent but it attributed the manifestation of the power of the Holy Spirit to Satan.

From the context we learn that the Lord Jesus had performed some miracles which caused the people to say, "Is not this the son of David?" (v. 23). The Pharisees realized that if Jesus were recognized as the Messiah they would lose their hold on the people, so they charged that Jesus' power was that of Beelzebub, the prince of demons. It was this which the Lord Jesus declared to be an unforgivable sin.

It may be noticed that this sin was committed deliberately, and with full knowledge of what they were doing. It is not a sin which can be committed inadvertently or in ignorance. Paul declares that he compelled people to blaspheme (Acts 26:9-11). Yet he says in I Timothy 1:13, "I obtained mercy, because I did it ignorantly in unbelief." This was not the case with these Pharisees. Their offense showed a state of hardened rebellion against God that would stop at nothing, not even blasphemy against the Holy Spirit. This is the unpardonable sin.

169. Can the sin of adultery be forgiven?

Many persons think of this as the unpardonable sin, but no sin against another human being is unpardonable, however serious it may be. In one sense *every* sin is against God. The prodigal son said, "I have sinned against heaven, and before thee" (Luke 15:18). Yet God makes only one sin unpardonable. This is a deliberate insult and blasphemy against the Holy Spirit.

We believe the Lord made this clear when He said in Matthew 12:31, "All manner of sin and blasphemy shall be forgiven unto

men: but the blasphemy against the Holy Ghost shall not be forgiven unto men." In view of this we should not consider any other
sin unforgivable.

Sometimes a person refuses to forgive another, especially if
the sin has been particularly injurious to the individual. This
scripture does not justify such an attitude, and makes it clear that
God Himself is willing to forgive all manner of sin. He only refuses to forgive the sin which constitutes deliberate rebellion
against Him.

170. Could the Lord Jesus Christ have sinned when He was tempted by Satan?

Many persons teach that if Christ could not have sinned, then
His temptation was not a valid one, and He is not, therefore, a
true example to us, since His circumstances were not the same
as ours. We believe this reasoning is not true and it is not according to Scripture.

We understand the Bible to teach that Jesus Christ was God
manifest in flesh (I Tim. 3:16). According to Philippians 2:5-11
He was subsisting in absolute deity, but He "took on him the form
of a servant." He did not divest Himself of His essential deity,
which I consider to be an impossibility. But He did divest Himself of the glory and privileges of deity, coming to the earth in
lowliness and meekness, subordinating His will entirely to that of
the Father. Since He was divine as well as human, it would not
have been possible for Him to sin.

It should be noticed that the Lord Jesus used His divine powers
for the benefit of others, but not for Himself. And He said, in
John 14:10, "The Father that dwelleth in me, he doeth the works,"
adding in verse 12, "Verily, verily I say unto you, He that believeth on me, the works that I do shall he do also; and greater
works than these shall he do, because I go to my Father." He did
not consider that His deity prevented His being an example of
what God could accomplish in those who believe on Him.

He met temptation not by a display of divine power but as any of us might. He answered Satan promptly and decisively from the Word of God. He did this while in physical weakness, after long fasting, not mitigated by His divine nature.

171. If Christ could not have sinned, how could His being tempted by Satan be a genuine temptation?

A test of purity does not imply the existence of impurity in the thing tested. When pure gold is given the acid test, it cannot be attacked by the acid used because the gold is pure. The purity of the gold does not make the test invalid, but the test proves that the gold was pure. So Satan's effort to tempt the Lord Jesus Christ not only brought proof that He was sinless but also demonstrated how anyone can resist sin.

When Satan approached Eve with a similar temptation, she was not prepared to resist him. In the case of the Lord Jesus, He was tempted at the end of forty days of fasting, and when He was "with the wild beasts" (Mark 1:13). Eve had not gone through a period of fasting, and she was surrounded by pleasant things. Yet when Satan approached her, instead of repeating what God had said, she added something to His words, omitted something, and distorted part of what He had said. Thus she became an easy prey to Satan's appeal.

A newly-built bridge is often tested by drawing over it a load heavier than engineers ever expect the bridge to bear. Such a test is designed primarily to demonstrate the known capacity of the bridge, not to find out if it can bear such a load. So the temptation of Christ demonstrated His inherent holiness, and it also showed how any person can defeat Satan. Christ's answer was immediate; He did not temporize. It was decisive; He did not waver. It was biblical. When anyone faces Satan with a confident "Thus saith the Lord," he will experience what is described in James 4:7: "Submit yourselves therefore to God. Resist the devil, and he will flee from you."

172. What is the willful sin referred to in Hebrews 10:26-29 which, if a person commits it, will result in his being lost?

Verses 26 and 27 mention the sin, while verses 28 and 29 give a comparison in which the sin is further amplified. "For if we sin wilfully after that we have received the knowledge of the truth, there remaineth no more sacrifice for sins, but a certain fearful looking for of judgment and fiery indignation, which shall devour the adversaries. He that despised Moses' law died without mercy under two or three witnesses: of how much sorer punishment, suppose ye, shall he be thought worthy, who hath trodden under foot the Son of God, and hath counted the blood of the covenant, wherewith he was sanctified, an unholy [or, common] thing, and hath done despite unto [insulted] the Spirit of grace?"

Here we see that the sin is a willful one; hence it is a deliberate rejection of Christ. The person is said to have "trodden under foot the Son of God." This verse is not speaking of falling into sins of immorality but of counting the blood of Christ "a common thing." A person who does this is saying that the shed blood of Christ has no more redeeming value than the blood of any other person.

Since this sin is deliberately committed, we take it to be similar to that referred to in chapter 6, where some who had espoused Christianity later purposefully rejected Him, thus "treading Him under foot." For such persons there is "no more sacrifice for sin." They have rejected the only sacrifice that can save. They share the "fiery indignation which shall devour the adversaries." We take it that these individuals never were truly saved, or born again.

173. Is sickness because of sin? I have been told God does not heal me because I am keeping something back from Him.

We believe it is unkind and cruel, and totally unscriptural, to tell handicapped persons that they are afflicted because of some unconfessed sin or disobedience to God. Some very godly persons have been lifelong invalids, while some persons who are total strangers to God have been healthy and strong, as well as many worldly-minded Christians. We cannot equate our physical state with our spiritual state. Psalm 73 gives a discussion of this, and the writer, Asaph, says of himself, because he had previously so judged, "So foolish was I, and ignorant: I was as a beast before thee" (v. 22).

It is true that sometimes a person experiences sickness because of some sin in his life. See for example, I Corinthians 11:30: "For this cause many are weak and sickly among you, and many sleep." But that this is not always the case is shown in James 5:15, where we are instructed to pray for the sick. James says, "And if he have committed sins, they shall be forgiven him." If sickness were the result of our coming short of God's will for our lives, most of us would be in poor health much of the time.

There is another aspect to suffering. I Corinthians 12:26 says, "And whether one member suffer, all the members suffer with it." Suffering is intended not only to draw the sufferer himself closer to the Lord but to awaken spiritual exercises in all of us, and to draw out our hearts in love toward one another.

174. If I have confessed all known sin and still have a "block" between me and God, how can I remove it?

If you have confessed all known sin in your life there is no "block" between you and God, assuming, of course, that you have forsaken the sin. Proverbs 28:13 says: "He that covereth his sins shall not prosper: but whoso confesseth and forsaketh them shall have mercy." If a Christian has confessed and forsaken sin, he is entitled to accept God's forgiveness as stated in I John 1:9, "If we confess our sins, he is faithful and just to forgive us our sins, and to cleanse us from all unrighteousness."

As Christians, the memory of our sins should keep us humble and should keep us ever "looking unto Jesus" for needed grace and strength to refrain from further sinning and to glorify Him in our lives. But it is a mistake to fail to recognize that God has forgiven our sins, so that we can again enjoy full communion with

Him. Of course, it may be that the sin has to do with a matter which requires restitution. If so, I believe Scripture teaches that such restitution should be made wherever possible.

Sometimes a person feels he should have some "sign" from God that He has forgiven him. However, Christians have what is better than any sign; they have His infallible, unchanging Word, and are entitled to rest in what it says. Otherwise Satan will gain an advantage over the Christian, and fruitfulness to God will be hindered.

175. What is the "sin unto death" mentioned in I John 5:16?

I John 5:16-17 says: "If any man see his brother sin a sin which is not unto death, he shall ask, and he shall give him life for them that sin not unto death. There is a sin unto death: I do not say that he shall pray for it. All unrighteousness is sin: and there is a sin not unto death." To understand these verses, we need to decide first of all, whether the word *death* refers to physical or spiritual death. If the word *death* refers to spiritual death, this verse would be teaching that it is possible for those possessing the eternal life of God to lose it. Further, if we discern that the sin is unto death, we are not to pray for the person committing it. To me, this view seems wrong in every aspect of it.

If physical death is referred to, then we have to decide whether it is death at the hands of men or of God. If the former, then the meaning would be, as some teach, that if a person has committed a capital crime we should never pray that he might escape the death sentence. But the context seems to me to be speaking rather of a dealing of God, not with regard to a capital crime, but with a course or condition of sin. Taken this way, the meaning is that in certain cases God deals with sin in the lives of His children by taking them away in death. A case in point is seen in I Corinthians 11:30, "For this cause many are weak and sickly among you, and many sleep."

The fact that no sin is named, nor even a category suggested, indicates that God does not necessarily always deal with a certain sin in the same way.

The one problem confronting one who takes this view is how one can know when a sin is to be considered a "sin unto death." Sometimes the person being so dealt with by God has the conviction that this is so, and will tell his friends not to pray for him. Other than this, we can only say it is a matter of one's own discernment. If we have the conviction that it is a sin unto death, then John is saying we should not interfere with what we recognize to be a dealing of God with the person.

176. Are some sins forgiven in the next world?

Scripture makes it very clear that "now is the accepted time; now is the day of salvation" (II Cor. 6:2). The idea of forgiveness in the world to come rests on the false assumption that men must expiate their sins by suffering, which cannot be done. The wages of sin is not suffering, but *death* (Rom. 6:23). This would involve eternal separation from God, and it is only because Christ suffered and died in our place that sin can be forgiven. If His death did not expiate all sin, we could not be saved; but if it did, then believers in Him are saved now and their sins are forgiven, as many scriptures state. (See, for instance, Acts 13:38-39.)

Sometimes inferences are drawn from certain passages which might seem to support the idea of forgiveness in the world to come. One such passage is Matthew 12:32: ". . . whosoever speaketh against the Holy Ghost, it shall not be forgiven him, neither in this world, neither in the world to come." In this verse the word *world* might more correctly be translated "age," and Jesus is not speaking of forgiveness in another world but is saying that this sin will not be forgiven in any *age*. That this statement is not intended to teach the forgiveness of sins in another world seems clear from Luke 16, where Jesus told of a certain man who "died, and was buried; and in hell he lift up his eyes, being in torments" (Luke 16:22-23). When he begged for some alleviation of his condition, he was told, "They which would pass from hence to you cannot; neither can they pass to us, that would come from thence" (v. 26). The Bible offers no hope of salvation after death.

In fact, the opposite is stated in Job 36:18-19: "Because there is wrath, beware lest he take thee away with his stroke: then a great ransom cannot deliver thee. Will he esteem thy riches? no, not gold, nor all the forces of strength."

SOVEREIGNTY OF GOD

177. What is meant by the sovereignty of God?

The term "sovereignty of God" is not found in the Bible, though the idea is. But since it is not a biblical term, it does not mean the same thing to all who use it. Lewis Sperry Chafer in his *Systematic Theology* says, "By many writers *sovereignty* is not included among the attributes of God. It is more properly a *prerogative* of God."

The word *sovereign* is derived from the Latin *super* ("above"), and indicates that God has absolute authority and power in His creation. He governs and controls all things according to His own thoughts and will, and is not accountable to anyone else. Men have engaged in considerable theological dispute as to how this applies to God's dealings with men. Some hold that God determines every act and decision of mankind, and that men are saved or lost by His choice.

Some holding this view have insisted that "whatever God permits, He willed or designed." This makes God accountable for everything that happens, whether good or evil. We believe this concept to be contrary to all that the Bible reveals of the character of God. Besides, this view seems to vitiate the atonement of Christ, for why should such a fearful price be paid for redemption from sins which God Himself caused to be committed?

We believe rather that in many areas of life God has given man the power of choice, though He determines the consequences of the choices man makes. This was exhibited in the garden of Eden, when Adam and Eve chose to disobey God. God did not accept responsibility for the choice they made, but laid the full penalty of it upon them, although, in His infinite grace, He offered a way of escape from that penalty by His promise of salvation.

179

178. How does the "sovereignty of God" apply to man's salvation?

Various views are held on this subject. Some hold that God decides, absolutely, who shall be saved and who shall be lost. The holders of this view believe God cannot be considered sovereign unless He makes every decision that is made, and unless the entire universe is at all times doing His will.

Others believe this to be a harsh view, not consonant with the love of God. They hold that while salvation is all of God and therefore none can be saved except by a sovereign act of God bringing it about without reference to any fact or feature about the person himself, yet it is the grace of God which operates to save any, and He is not obligated to save all. Hence His love is expressed in the salvation of some, while His sovereignty is expressed in not saving all.

My own view differs from these, but coincides with that of those who believe that as God gave man, in the garden of Eden, the choice to obey or disobey His commandment, so now He gives men the choice of submitting to Christ, receiving Him by faith as their Lord and Saviour, or of refusing to do so. We are told in I Peter 1:2 that God made His choice (or "election") on the basis of His foreknowledge, so that He did not have to wait until man's choice was made to be able to make His selection.

Had God reserved the choice for Himself, we are told He would have chosen every one. I Timothy 2:4 says, God ". . . will have all men to be saved, and to come unto the knowledge of the truth." II Peter 3:9 states this truth negatively: "The Lord is . . . long-suffering to us-ward, not willing that any should perish, but that all should come to repentance." But while God gives man the power of choice, He in His sovereign right has set the terms on which He will receive man: "the obedience of faith" (Rom. 16:26).

179. If "God is love," how can He send people to hell?

God is not only "love"; He is also "light, and in him is no darkness at all" (I John 1:5). The prophet Habakkuk, speaking to
God, said, "Thou art of purer eyes than to behold evil, and canst
not look on iniquity." A holy God could never tolerate sin, or a
sinful person, in His presence.

But it is not only sin which results in men being cast into hell;
it is more directly their attitude toward God's Son. In view of the
fact that the infinite God who made us gave His Son to be our
Saviour, the greatest insult and act of rebellion against God that
man could commit is to reject this "unspeakable gift." When one
does so, I do not see that we need to justify God in sending such
a person to hell.

It may be noticed that in Revelation 20, where we read of the
final judgment of unsaved persons, their being cast into the lake
of fire was based on the fact that their names were not found
written in the Book of Life. That is, they had never received
Jesus Christ as their Saviour. Their *works* determine the degree
or measure of their judgment.

180. If there is a God, why does He allow suffering and evil?

This question can be considered philosophically and morally.
A universe in which no evil were possible would have required a
creation in which no one except God had the power to choose.
But God desired the companionship of a creature with the power
of choice (Gen. 1:26-27; 3:6-13). This involved the possibility of
such a creature making a wrong choice. Otherwise, men would
have been like robots. An automobile will obey every desire of
its owner, but most men prefer the companionship of a wife even
though she does not always respond to her husband's wishes.

Morally, God might have blotted out sin at its inception, but
had He intended to do this, it is not likely that He would have
given His creatures the power of choice at all. Instead, God met
the problem by sending His Son into the world to be our Saviour.
This gives every man the privilege of making his own choice with

regard to his eternal destiny. Those who submit to God in the obedience of faith (Rom. 16:26) are received by Him and cleansed from sin on the ground of Christ's atonement.

In the meantime, God allows men to continue making their choices within the limits of His providential overruling. He governs the circumstances of men in such a way that they reap the fruit of their doings, and those who are His children learn many lessons of grace and faith which cannot be learned in heaven. In addition, we have His promise that "all things work together for good to them that love God, to them who are the called according to his purpose" (Rom. 8:28). Taken singly, various circumstances might not seem to be working for our good, but taken together, they prove to be for our good. In the Book of Genesis we find an excellent example of this in the history of Joseph, the son of Jacob.

181. How can we answer one who asked when a little child was killed in an accident, "Where was God?"

Anyone who has lost a loved one in an accident would feel the poignancy of this question which is part of the age-old question of why the righteous or innocent are allowed to suffer. The answer takes us back to the beginning of human experience. Sin involved a twofold penalty: spiritual death, and physical death. Adam and Eve died spiritually as soon as they sinned, and they became subject to physical death. Instead of God's inflicting physical death by a sudden stroke of His power, He caused a "law of death" to begin to work in their bodies. Adam did not die until 930 years later (Gen. 5:5).

Had God cut them off physically, it would have meant casting them into outer darkness, and the human race would have ended where it started. Had God done that, it seems unlikely that He would have created humanity at all. Instead, God allowed Adam and Eve to live for a time physically, and offered them salvation through faith in a coming Saviour. In our case, of course, the Saviour *has* come, so now it is our privilege to believe in the Saviour who lived, and died an atoning death, and rose again from the dead, and is now seated at God's right hand. But the basic principle is the same: salvation is always "by grace . . . through faith" (Eph. 2:8-9).

But the longsuffering of God involves allowing man still to do according to his own will, except that God sets overall limits to prevent absolute chaos. And in His providence He so orders things that, taken together, "all things work together for good to them that love God, to them who are the called according to his purpose" (Rom. 8:28). But God does this with two limitations: (1) God allows men to do what they will. If He were not willing to do so now, why should He have done so in the beginning, when Adam and Eve fell into sin? This was the nature of man: God gave him the power of choice (though not of consequences attending his choices). Hence a believer may temporarily suffer from injustice at the hand of his fellows. (2) Since the sin of man brought also a curse upon the earth (Gen. 3:17), this involved a disruption of nature, which brings hardships to all men. All of this serves to discipline men of faith, and God often allows those who are rebellious against Him to reap the fruit of their sins.

However, the providences of God are often applied indiscriminately, whether for good or ill. In Matthew 5:45-48 the Lord Jesus says that God "maketh his sun to rise on the evil and on the good, and sendeth rain on the just and on the unjust." Likewise, when accidents and epidemics occur, they are not restricted to the unbelieving and sinful. The compensations of faith and righteousness are not always received in this world, but they are assured in the world to come.

The first death recorded in the Bible was that of Abel, murdered by his brother Cain. Where was God then? Where was God when the Christian martyrs were being tortured to death in the early days of this era? Where is He when His people suffer in the present day? Someone has replied, "Exactly where He was when His Son suffered cruel tortures and was crucified." While the overruling providence of God does sometimes deliver His children from adverse circumstances, as in the case of Daniel in the lions' den and in the case of his three companions in the fiery furnace, He does not always do so; and even these were prepared to die, should God so will.

An interesting consideration is raised in Isaiah 57:1, where we read, "The righteous perisheth, and no man layeth it to heart: and merciful men are taken away, none considering that the righteous is taken away from the evil to come." If we knew a person were going to have a life of deep sorrow and suffering, would we not be glad if God took him away in childhood? Sometimes people complain when an old person is allowed to linger, especially if suffering or incapacity is involved. Often, what we want is all the good of life, and none of the ill,.

The question resolves itself to this: Do we believe that there is a God, and that He is over all things? Are we willing to trust His wisdom, love, and power in all things? If God were to deal with wicked people now, He would deal with all of us, for "there is no difference, for all have sinned, and come short of the glory of God" (Rom. 3:23). Usually men want God to deal with the sin of others, but not their own. For God to prevent all accidents would mean He would have to regulate not only nature but all the acts and decisions of men. This would nullify His purpose in creating man with the power of choice.

Having had the experience of losing my father when I was a child, my mother being left a widow with six small children, and having experienced other such losses within our immediate family, I have lived long enough to know that God does not abandon those who trust in Him. There are compensations in life, as well as sufferings, but there are intricacies which go beyond our powers of explanation. God's Word teaches that the issues of life will be seen more clearly in eternity. Various experiences, if measured by this world, defy explanation; but if we take eternity into account, we can have "peace, perfect peace, in this dark world of sin" because "the blood of Jesus whispers peace within."

SPIRIT BEINGS

182. When and how did Satan come into being?

If, as we take it, Satan is a fallen angel, then the question involves two considerations: (1) How and when did angels come into being? (2) When and how did he become the adversary of God?

With regard to the first, it appears that angels were created simultaneously with the universe itself. We take it that the phrase "in the beginning" (Gen. 1:1) indicates the origin of any form of existence besides God. If this be true, then no created being could have existed before this time, and so angels could not have antedated the universe.

In Job 38 God asked Job some interesting questions, among which were these: "Where wast thou when I laid the foundations of the earth? . . . When the morning stars sang together, and all the sons of God shouted for joy?" (vv. 4-7). If, as some think, light waves, in addition to making things visible, can be heard, then the first part of verse 7 might be taken literally as it stands, although many consider it figurative. But the second part of the verse clearly refers to some created intelligence. There are many reasons for believing that this refers, not to men, who were created long afterward, but to angels.

If the foregoing is correct, then the creation of angels must have been coincident with that of the universe. But it is self-evident that God did not create a competitor to Himself, and so we must conclude that Satan was created in a perfect state, and that he became Satan (which means "adversary") by an act of rebellion against God. The fact that he is called "the prince of the power of the air," and has demons under his control, indicates that some of the angelic host joined him in his rebellion.

183. If Satan was created perfect, how could he sin? Also, where in the Bible do we read of this?

The fact that any beings are created in a perfect state does not mean they cannot sin, if they are created with the power of choice, as was true with both men and angels. The nature of Christ was different, because in Him deity was combined with humanity, so that He was not only perfect in His being but had an intrinsic holiness which resisted sin. While Scripture does not give us an account of the creation of Satan, there are two passages which are believed by many Bible students to refer to him, and which give us an idea of his original purity and of what led to his fall into sin.

One of these passages is Ezekiel 28:11-17. While the entire passage speaks of the "prince of Tyrus" (v. 2), yet it seems also to refer to a being who was more than a mere man, and what is said could only be applied to the earthly king of Tyre in a graphic, figurative sense. But if we take what is said as applying to Satan, we learn that he was "full of wisdom and perfect in beauty," as originally created. The passage also indicates that his original assignment was upon earth. And the statement, "Thou wast perfect in thy ways from the day that thou was created till iniquity was found in thee" would indicate that, though created perfect, he became the originator of sin.

The second of these passages is Isaiah 14:12-15, which, if we take it to refer to him, describes the nature of his sin. The entire passage refers to the king of Babylon, but there are reasons for believing that Satan identifies himself with whoever is the leading political power in the world at a given time. If this be so, it is easy to see how he might be described as the king of Tyre at one time, and the king of Babylon at another. The Lord Jesus three times referred to him as "the prince of this world" (John 12:31; 14:30; 16:11). Scripture indicates that the affairs of nations are affected by the activities of both angels and demons.

Taking this passage in Isaiah to refer to Satan, we see that he felt his assignment in connection with the earth was too trivial for his status, which may well have been that of archangel, or prince of the angels. He is referred to as "Lucifer, son of the morning." The word *Lucifer* means "shining one," or "light-bearer." As a created being and a servant of God, he was not informed of his Master's plans concerning the earth (cf. John 15:15), and therefore did not understand the importance of it as the sphere where God would display Himself both in His creature, man, created in His own image and likeness (Gen. 1:26), and later, in the incarnation of His own Son.

In the five "I will's" of verses 13-14 we see the root of all sin, which is the setting of one's own mind and will against that of God. There is also the impugning of God's love and wisdom, as though He either did not know what was best for us, or was unwilling to give it to us. God's will is always the highest good His wisdom can devise. In the garden of Eden Satan succeeded in convincing man he could do better for himself than God had planned for him; and this is a contemporary problem in the world today.

184. **Will you discuss God and his angels, and Satan and his angels? Also, is there any way of knowing the comparative numbers of each?**

A term is used of spirit beings, "principalities and powers," which sometimes refers to the holy angels, sometimes to the demonical powers, and sometimes to both. Satan is called "the prince of the power of the air" (Eph. 2:2), and it appears that both his hosts and the holy angels are organized in keeping with earthly kingdoms. In Daniel 10 we find references to "the prince of Persia: and . . . the prince of Grecia" (v. 20); both are in a context which indicates that spirit beings are referred to. The fact that the angel sent to Daniel had to fight against them marks them as *evil* spirits, or fallen angels.

Also, the reference in Daniel 11:1 to the fact this angel was active in the first year of Darius shows that angels have a part in the affairs of men, and in the course of empires. It is not altogether clear whether the pronoun "him" in 11:1 refers to Michael, whom this angel (presumably Gabriel) helped, or whether it refers to Darius. In either case, it indicates angelic intervention in the affairs of men and nations.

All of this implies that, in the government of the earth, God has His angels organized in principalities and powers, and Satan does also. These forces, though unseen, evidently come into conflict, and such conflict seems to have a determinative effect on the course of events. It may be noticed that Michael, called the archangel (Jude 9), is said to stand in a special way for the children of Israel (Dan. 12:1).

As to the comparative numbers of angels in the hosts of God and of Satan, there is no way to ascertain this. Some have thought from reading the statement in Revelation 12:4, about the dragon who with his tail drew the third part of the stars of heaven, that there are therefore a third as many fallen angels as there are holy ones. But we do not see in this passage any reference to Satan's original rebellion against God. The statement is probably figurative, relating to Satan's control at that time over the great men of the earth.

In Matthew 26:53 the Lord Jesus speaks of "more than twelve legions of angels," but perhaps the most specific statement of the number of angels is given in Daniel 7:10, where we read, "thousand thousands ministered unto him, and ten thousand times ten thousand ministered before him." While these numbers are not specific, they reveal that while millions of angels are engaged in the service of God, hundreds of millions stand in reserve, awaiting His bidding. It is very doubtful that Satan has a third as many under his control, although the number is evidently quite large.

185. What is the place of angels in God's plan?

There is no detailed description of angels in the Bible, but we read many things about them which give us a concept of their place in creation. That they are a distinct order of beings seems clear from such statements as that found in Psalm 8:5 concerning man: "Thou hast made him a little lower than the angels." Psalm

103:20 says, "Bless the LORD, ye his angels, that excel in strength, that do his commandments, hearkening unto the voice of his word."

Many scriptures indicate that angels are spirit beings, as Hebrews 1:14 explicitly states. The word *angel* means "messenger," and sometimes is used in that sense without reference to an angelic being. But this usage reveals one of their important functions, since on many occasions angels were used to communicate messages from God to men. Acts 7:53, together with Hebrews 2:2, indicates that Moses received the law through the mediation of angels. *Communication* is suggested by their "ascending and descending" (Gen. 28:12; John 1:51).

In Psalm 34:7 we are told that "the angel of the LORD encampeth round about them that fear him, and delivereth them." So we see that one element of the service of angels is the protection of the children of God. From Matthew 4:11 we learn that they ministered to Christ at the conclusion of His temptation in the wilderness. It was an angel who released Peter from prison (Acts 12:7-11). Psalm 91:11 makes a general statement along this line.

Angels also sometimes execute the judgments of God, as when the angel stood with a drawn sword in the way of Balaam (Numbers 22). Also, the Lord indicated in His parable of the wheat and tares that it will be the angels who will remove from His kingdom the evil elements which would pollute it (Matt. 13:41, 49-50). Angels are also said to be spectators of what we do, as in I Corinthians 4:9 and Ephesians 3:10. Daniel 7:10 indicates that besides those which are called into activity, a much larger host of angels are held in reserve. See also Matthew 26:53. It would be impossible to enumerate the many and varied ways in which angels serve the will of God, but I would point out that they also praise Him as their Creator (Psalm 148:2).

186. How can we determine, when we experience trouble, whether it is the result of Satan's power or is allowed to come to us by the will of God?

We learn from many scriptures that nothing comes to the child of God except by His permission. Consequently, even if Satan is allowed to attack us, we are justified in taking the event as from the hand of God.

We see an example of this in the life of Job. God asked Satan what he thought of Job. Satan challenged God to withdraw His blessings from Job, saying that Job would then curse God. Then God gave Satan permission to attack Job, with this limitation: "Upon himself put not forth thine hand" (1:12). Satan promptly brought upon Job a number of disasters, beginning with the loss of his large herds of livestock, by which the wealth of those days was measured. He also took the life of Job's ten children at one stroke. Job's response to all this was, "The LORD gave, and the LORD hath taken away; blessed be the name of the LORD" (1:21).

Job might have argued that these troubles were the work of an enemy, and that Satan was the cause. This would have been correct; but he also knew God had permitted these troubles or they would not have happened. Later Satan obtained permission to attack Job's person, but again God set a limit: Satan was not to take Job's life. Satan at once brought upon Job an affliction of "sore boils from the sole of his foot to his crown" (2:7). Again Job looked beyond Satan as the immediate cause of his trouble, and said, "Shall we receive good at the hand of God, and shall we not receive evil [i.e., adversity]?" He took it as from God, even though the immediate cause was Satan.

In I Thessalonians 2:18 Paul says, of a certain situation, "Satan hindered," acknowledging him as the source of the difficulty. On another occasion we are told "the Spirit suffered them not" (Acts 16:7), and from this statement we learn that God's purposes are not frustrated by any act of Satan. However, the latter reference may mean that Paul had an inward conviction by the Spirit. The statement is valid in either case.

Psalm 76:10 sheds light on this question: "Surely the wrath of man shall praise thee; the remainder of wrath shalt thou restrain." God only permits that which He can turn into blessing and through which He can accomplish His purposes. "The remainder of wrath shalt thou restrain."

We read in Mark 9:22 how the father of a boy possessed by a demon said, "Ofttimes it hath cast him into the fire, and into the waters, to destroy him." From this verse we learn that Satan's power, exercised in this case by the demon, had the purpose of destruction. But Psalm 66:12 shows how God overrules when Satan's purpose is destruction: "We went through fire and through water, but thou broughtest us out into a wealthy place." In spite of Satan's intention God uses the circumstances for blessing. Job, at the end of the troubles God permitted in his life, emerged with "twice as much as he had before" (Job 42:10).

187. Do you believe angels are seen of men today? Might an angel appear as a man on the street and talk to me?

I would say that ordinarily angels are *not* seen by men today, but I would not be absolute in that statement. It appears in the Old Testament that God on several occasions dealt with men through angels used as intermediaries. In such cases the angels appeared as young men. But this dispensation is not characterized by such appearances. We have the completed Word of God and the indwelling presence of the Holy Spirit. No doubt angels watch over us (Heb. 1:14), but I do not think it likely that they would appear to men and talk with them.

Highly impressionable persons sometimes have hallucinations, and sometimes stories are circulated which have no foundation in fact. And while it is true that missionaries, working in primitive circumstances, have occasionally had experiences which are out of the ordinary, even a missionary can be impressionable and relate a story which is easily enlarged and embellished. Such a story can be used to support the idea, when actually it is not factual.

Yet the fact that such manifestations have been recorded in Scripture prevents one from saying they could not happen. One story about angels which seems to be authentic had to do with the well-known missionary to the New Hebrides, John G. Paton. Since he had aroused the enmity of the local chief by his successes in the gospel, a man was hired to kill the missionary. The man went to the missionary's house but instead of murdering Mr. Paton he returned in terror, saying he had seen a row of men dressed in white surrounding the missionary's home. The chief thought the man had drunk too much whiskey, and encouraged him to try again. The next time others of the tribe accompanied him. That night they all saw three rows of men surrounding Paton's home.

When the chief asked the missionary where he kept the men in daytime who surrounded his house at night, he, knowing nothing of what had happened, disclaimed the whole idea. When the chief, in amazement, told his story, the missionary realized they had seen an angelic company which God had sent to protect him, and he related it to Psalm 34:7, "The angel of the Lord encampeth round about them that fear him, and delivereth them." The savages were powerfully impressed with the missionary's explanation, as well they might be.

In this case, the missionary himself did not see the angels; and they did not communicate any revelation from God. Their presence was a manifestation to those who were enemies of Christ and to the missionary of the protecting power of God. This incident sounds authentic to me, but I have heard stories of angelic manifestation which did not sound authentic.

188. Please explain Luke 11:24-26.

In these verses we read that the Lord Jesus said, "When the unclean spirit is gone out of a man, he walketh through dry places seeking rest; and finding none, he saith, I will return unto my house whence I came out. And when he cometh, he findeth it swept and garnished. Then goeth he, and taketh to him seven other spirits more wicked than himself; and they enter in, and dwell there: and the last state of that man is worse than the first."

The Lord Jesus was evidently describing reformation of life without the experience of regeneration. The passage is very similar to the two parables by which Peter illustrates the same truth (II Pet. 2:20-22). People, through knowledge of the truth of God and of the gospel, clean up their lives, but do not come to Christ in repentance and faith, which would result in the new birth. The evil spirit which before dominated the person later returns and, liking the new condition of things, takes seven spirits more wicked than himself, and all enter in and dwell there, making the person's last end worse than his original sinful state.

Many consider these words of Jesus to have also a prophetical bearing. A nation which, through the judgments of God, puts away idolatry and acknowledges Him, but fails to receive the Lord Jesus Christ as Lord and Saviour, is open to believe the lie of the antichrist when he comes. See John 5:43, where Jesus said, "I am come in my Father's name, and ye receive me not: if another shall come in his own name, him ye will receive."

It should be noted that no nation of people acts as a unit, and in any nation there are those who believe and those who do not. But the nation is characterized by the attitude of the majority of its members, and so God deals with nations, not overlooking faith wherever it exists in any individual.

SPORTS AND AMUSEMENTS

189. Should I give up listening to ball games? I enjoy listening to them, and if I were to deny myself this pleasure, it would be a real sacrifice. Yet the Bible tells us we should not love the world, nor the things which are in the world. I know that listening to ball games distracts from the Lord.

In dealing with such questions one is tempted to answer categorically either "Yes" or "No," but such answers are not necessarily either the most scriptural or the most spiritual. What might be perfectly proper for one person may not be at all wise for another. We cannot say that ball games, or watching or listening to them, are essentially wrong. Many Christians do both, and do not feel they have weakened either their communion with the Lord or their witness for Him.

Scripture gives us these principles: "Whether therefore ye eat, or drink, or whatsoever ye do, do all for the glory of God" (I Cor. 10:31) and "Whatsoever is not of faith is sin" (Rom. 14:23). Among Christians we find differing degrees of light and spiritual experience, and what affects one adversely does not necessarily affect another in the same way. In matters of conscience, each person must be guided by the Holy Spirit, so that he acts in the conviction of faith and in the confidence that he is pleasing God, whether his decision be positive or negative.

To bind the lives and consciences of others by one's personal convictions is neither scriptural nor spiritual; it is tyranny. But if a person finds an activity distracts from the Lord, then for that person it is wrong. Sometimes it is a question of the amount of time or money given to it, or both. But other considerations may enter into one's decision. In many cases there does not seem to be any good reason why a person should not enjoy watching or listening to a contest which is a clean sport, carried on under conditions which do not compromise a Christian's testimony.

Since a decision on such a question must be based on principle rather than precept, each person must be led by the Holy Spirit as he prayerfully considers all that is involved in the matter. He may then feel free to do what others may think to be wrong for them. Let us avoid judging one another, and, on the basis of Roman 14, let us maintain genuine Christian regard for one another whether we reach the same conclusion or not.

190. Is it wrong for a Christian to engage in sports? Is it wrong for a Christian to be a professional in this field?

In I Timothy 4:8 the Apostle Paul wrote: "For bodily exercise profiteth little [or, for a little]: but godliness is profitable unto all things, having promise of the life that now is, and of that which is to come." This verse, while indicating that godliness is far more important than physical exercise, does not therefore disparage physical exercise. In saying, in the better rendering, that it "profiteth *for* a little," the comparison has to do with time, in contrast with eternity.

We do not consider physical sports wrong, especially for young people, unless there are accompanying circumstances detrimental to spiritual standards. When people become older, sports usually give way to physical work. Many persons become incapacitated for strenuous sports as years pass by. Many find that in giving themselves to Christian activities they have less time for sports, not because they are wrong but as having only a passing value.

We see nothing essentially wrong in a person's taking up some form of sports as a livelihood, if he does not violate Scripture in the pursuit of such a course, nor do we see that Scripture is violated in a person's maintaining an interest in sports, and witnessing them, if he does not allow this to keep him back from proper spiritual exercises.

191. Are Sunday sports wrong for a professional, since he is earning a living? What about playing golf on Sunday?

An answer to the question of Sunday sports rests on our view of what God expects of us in connection with the Lord's Day. We believe we are not under the law of Moses, although we must recognize that because God's moral character never changes His children are never free to indulge in sin in any form. Though we do not believe we are under the sabbath law, we do believe that God intends not only that we should observe one day in seven as a "work break," but that we should devote that day to His service.

While Isaiah 58:13-14 refers to Israel's sabbath, yet we believe these verses give us guidelines for observing any day in which we desire especially to honor God. "If thou turn away thy foot from the sabbath, from doing thy pleasure on my holy day; and call the sabbath a delight, the holy of the LORD, honorable; and shalt honor him, not doing thine own ways, nor finding thine own pleasure, nor speaking thine own words. . . ." While, as we have said, this relates directly to the sabbath, we believe that it also gives some guidelines for the observance of the Lord's Day. This would apply to non-professional as well as to professional sports.

We do not try to regulate the lives of others, recognizing that each must give account of himself to God. Yet if we recognize that we are in this world to witness for Christ, we shall judge the propriety of any act of ours on the basis of whether it helps or hinders our efforts to win others to Him. What manner of life do we expect our missionaries to lead? What would we think of them if they lived as we do? Do we expect more of them than the Lord expects of us?

We recognize that missionaries often live under cultural conditions different from ours, and the same rules would not always apply to both. But the same *principle* will govern both: "Whether therefore ye eat, or drink, or whatsoever ye do, do all to the glory of God" (I Cor. 10:31). Let us not judge one another, for we are commanded not to do so. Let us watch and pray and witness for Christ, and if we disagree with others, be much in prayer

for them, and provoke them to love and good works by our own
example.

192. **What can a Christian child who believes dancing is wrong
for a Christian do when he is required to take social dancing in school?**

The *way* such a problem is met may mean more to the child
than is now realized, because many similar, but greater, problems will be met later in life. The way we meet daily problems
forms our character. It is difficult for a young child to stand
against the trend of society, especially when enforced by the
authorities above him. But we find in the Bible a similar case,
which may serve as a guide here. I refer to Daniel the prophet.

We do not know the age of the young captives taken to Babylon, but it is generally believed they may have been fifteen to
eighteen years of age, quite possibly the lower figure. According
to Daniel 1 they found themselves in a position where they were
required to partake of "a daily provision of the king's meat, and of
the wine which he drank." Apart from the question of alcoholic
beverages, it seems likely that the food had been dedicated to an
idol. Whatever his reasons, Daniel felt he should not partake of it.

We read in verse 8 that "Daniel purposed in his heart that he
would not defile himself with the portion of the king's meat, nor
with the wine which he drank." It might have been "fit for the
king," but not for this young Hebrew, a believer in the living
God. Even though a refusal to eat and drink what the king provided might have resulted in his being executed, Daniel requested
that he and his companions might be excused from partaking.
In this case, they were excused; but in somewhat similar circumstances Daniel's three companions were condemned to death by
being cast into a fiery furnace when they refused to bow down
to an image the emperor had made (Daniel 3). This appears
also to have been in their youth, but from chapter 6 we learn that
Daniel showed the same courage almost 70 years later.

In a case where Christian parents back up the child, they can
appeal to the teacher, or the principal, if necessary, and take

whatever steps are possible to obtain the child's release from the requirement to take social dancing. Usually this is not forced upon the child, though the child can be humiliated by an antagonistic teacher. In many cases the convictions of the child and his parents are respected.

193. **Why should dancing be considered wrong when we read of it in the Old Testament? Psalm 150:4 says, "Praise him with the timbrel and dance." Also, there was dancing when the prodigal son returned home (Luke 15:25).**

The first mention of combining music and song in the worship of God seems to be Exodus 15:20, where Miriam and the women of Israel replied to the song of Moses with a kind of chorus, using timbrels (or tambourines) to accompany the music, while they also danced. This was not social dancing, and there was no mingling of men and women.

From the time of David, music became part of worship (II Sam. 6:15; I Chron. 23:5; 25:1-6), and was adopted into the Temple service from its first establishment (II Chron. 5:12). The New Testament says nothing about the use of music in the church unless I Corinthians 14:7 be considered an obscure reference to it. But that passage seems to be speaking more of music in general. Revelation 5:8 and 14:2-3 speak of musical accompaniment in heaven. For most of the church, the use of music in worship has not been repugnant, although some groups do not permit it.

"Dancing, on the contrary," says Ellicott's Commentary, "though adopted into religious worship by many nations, sanctioned by the present passage [Exodus 15:20], by the example of David (II Sam. 6:16), and by expressions in the Psalms (149:3; 150:4), has never found an entrance into Christian ceremonial, unless among a few fanatic sects. The reason of this is to be found in the abuses which, through human infirmity, became by degrees connected with the practice, causing it to become unfit for a religious purpose. In the primitive times, however, solemn and stately dances were deemed appropriate to festival periods and religious rejoicings, and among the more moral tribes and nations had nothing unseemly about them."

To summarize, we may note:

1) In the cases of the dancing led by Miriam (Exodus 15) and the dancing in which David participated (II Sam. 6), mixed groups were not involved; men and women were separated. The same was true of the kind of dancing described in Judges 21:19-21; apparently men normally were not present.

2) The dancing was in many cases spontaneous, to express their unbounded joy, and only their purity of motive kept it from becoming indecent, as seems clear from David's answer to the criticism voiced by his wife. However, this illustrates something of the danger of even such dancing, which was intended to glorify God and not to gratify any fleshly desire.

3) Where purity of motive and devotion to God were not the chief characteristics, the dancing soon degenerated into sin, as can be seen from Exodus 32:6, 19, 25.

4) Dancing, though practiced to a degree, was not incorporated into any divinely appointed ritual.

5) Apart from direct references to dancing, the ethics of Christianity teach separation from a social custom which, if not usually corrupt, easily lends itself to moral collapse. Dancing can be dangerous, and even disastrous, spiritually. We believe the Christian will make no mistake in keeping clear of it. There is no record in Scripture of dancing with persons of the opposite sex and no suggestion in the New Testament of any dancing in the spiritual exercises of the church.

194. Are amusements wrong for a Christian? Why can't I attend the theater, or go to a school dance?

The word "amusements" is used generally for that which entertains us or diverts our minds from the more serious things of life. I do not know of any precise limits for the word. It has been used of the theater, and also of sports of various kinds. The word covers a wide range of activities, too wide to discuss fully here. However, I will discuss certain aspects of the subject.

God has endowed man with a sense of humor, which is universal. In view of the many tensions which arise in this world of sin, we believe humor is often a saving grace so far as human relationships are concerned. An evening of music and conversation, or perhaps recitations could be considered entertainment, and could serve a very useful purpose of physical as well as mental relaxation.

Many Christians go in for physical exercises of various kinds: golf, tennis, swimming, boating, fishing, bowling, or other sports. We do not think that any of these is essentially wrong for a Christian, though some of them might sometimes involve an undesirable environment. This should be avoided lest one be thought to be engaging in unchristian activities.

I Timothy 4:8 says, "Bodily exercise profiteth little [or, for a little]: but godliness is profitable unto all things, having promise of the life that now is, and of that which is to come." Our body is the temple of the Holy Spirit, and it is right that it should be cared for and developed. But this should never be at the expense of "godliness," which is more important.

Not only should we avoid doing things which are defiling to our bodies and refuse to allow relaxation or exercise to take us into ungodly environments but we should also be on the alert lest we give the physical a place in our lives which would crowd out the spiritual. We need to give consideration to the time we devote to these things, the money we spend on them, and the degree to which we allow our minds to become occupied with them. There are many ways in which we can lose out spiritually for something which, while not wrong, is of lesser value than the things of eternity.

In going to the theater we are leaving it to others to direct the course of the entertainment offered, and often it is something less than edifying. Also, one's surroundings in such places usually are not conducive to spiritual thoughts or actions. The great majority of people there are not followers of the Lord Jesus Christ. In the area of "movies," especially, the industry has been characterized by the condoning of a very low standard of morals, both on the part of many actors and in many of the films produced. Going to such shows helps to support the industry.

Social dancing often excites fleshly desires which can easily lead to taking liberties which would not be taken at other times. Also one may submit to minor indignities while dancing which can be followed later by more overt acts. Since various forms of social dancing have been at times a prelude to immorality, it would seem that a believer would want to seek more spiritual ways of social pleasure.

TRINITY

195. Where does the Bible mention the Holy Trinity?

There is no direct statement in the Bible that God subsists as a Holy Trinity, but this is implied. Divine attributes are attributed to Father, Son, and Holy Spirit; and the Three are united in such verses as Matthew 28:19; II Corinthians 13:14; and many others. No created being could be associated with God the Father on an equal basis as is the Son. Hebrews 1:3 describes the Son as the One who, "being the brightness of his glory, and the express image of his person, and upholding all things by the word of his power, when he had by himself purged our sins, sat down on the right hand of the Majesty on high." No created being upholds all things by the word of his power, nor could any created being ever sit down at God's right hand on equality with Him.

It has been noticed that never has the name of a created being been associated with that of God, but the name of the Lord Jesus is frequently associated with the name of God the Father. One example of such association is Ephesians 1:2: "Grace be unto you, and peace, from God the Father, and the Lord Jesus Christ." Never is the name of any prophet or angel associated with that of the Father in this way.

But we are not left to inference alone. Both Jesus Christ and the Holy Spirit are called "God" in the Bible. See, for example, John 1:1-3, 14: "In the beginning was the Word, and the Word was with God, and the Word was God. The same was in the beginning with God. All things were made by him; and without him was not anything made that was made. . . . And the Word became flesh, and dwelt among us, (and we beheld his glory, the glory as of the only begotten of the Father,) full of grace and truth." See also Acts 5, where we read that Ananias and Sapphira lied to the Holy Ghost (v. 3), but were told by the Apostle Peter that they had lied to God (v. 4). Thus we see that Peter believed in the absolute deity of the Holy Spirit.

To the best of my knowledge, the first plain revelation of the Holy Trinity was at the baptism of the Lord Jesus. On that occasion, when He came out of the waters of baptism, the Holy Spirit descended upon Him in the form of a dove, and the Father spoke from heaven, saying, "This is my beloved Son, in whom I am well pleased." (See Matt. 3:16-17.) Looking back, we can see many implications of this truth in the Old Testament, but we believe it was first fully and clearly revealed at this time. The doctrine of the Trinity runs throughout the Bible, and does not rest on a single verse.

196. Does not the New Testament doctrine of the Holy Trinity deny the Old Testament teaching that there is one God?

We should be very clear about the fact that God never changes, though His methods of dealing with men may change in different ages or dispensations. But the essential nature and being of God are unchangeable. It is false to assume that the Old Testament reveals one God who is a God of vengeance while the New Testament reveals three Gods who are kind and loving. God was always a God of love and of infinite righteousness, and He is the same today. He was always a triune God, even though the fact was not so clearly revealed in the Old Testament as in the New.

We are told in Romans 1 that when men knew God they glorified Him not as God, but preferred a life of sin. This led to idolatry, and gradually the true knowledge of God was lost to men, and they began to ascribe deity to animals and the forces of nature, as well as to celestial bodies. They soon had a multiplicity of gods—a god for the mountains, another for the valleys; one for rivers and one for the fields; one for the wind, and another for the rain. They had gods for every occasion and circumstance. The Old Testament emphasized the existence of one God, who made heaven and earth and all things, ourselves included. Such emphasis on the fact of there being one God does not describe the nature of God.

In the New Testament this one God is clearly revealed as a triune Being, consisting of Father, Son, and Holy Spirit. This New Testament revelation is not inconsistent with the Old Testament emphasis on the fact that there is one God.

The *Shema,* Israel's often repeated declaration of faith, is found in Deuteronomy 6:4: "Hear, O Israel: The LORD our God is one LORD." Of this text the *New Bible Commentary* says: "The word employed here for 'one' (*eḥadh*) does not preclude the Christian concept of a trinity of persons within that unity; another word (*yaḥidh*) is used for the atomic unit of a monad, the barren Islamic idea which does not admit of a divine partnership." The word used can mean "united."

The New Testament does not teach three Gods. See, for example, I Timothy 2:5: "For there is one God, and one Mediator between God and men, the man Christ Jesus." The description of God's essential being is the same in both Testaments, as is also the description of His character and attributes. While the New Testament presents a fuller revelation of the nature and being of God through the incarnation of His Son, Jesus Christ our Lord, there is no conflict between the two revelations.

197. Does I Corinthians 15:27-28 mean that the Holy Trinity will then become one?

These verses say: "For he hath put all things under his feet. But when he saith all things are put under him, it is manifest that he is excepted, which did put all things under him. And when all things shall be subdued unto him, then shall the Son also himself be subject unto him that put all things under him, that God may be all in all."

I do not understand these verses to mean that God will ever cease to be a trinity. This is the nature of His being, and it is unalterable. Nor do I understand this passage to mean that Christ will then give up the humanity which He took in incarnation. The very statement that the Son shall Himself be subject to the Father seems to argue against that thought.

Many Bible students consider that this passage may be illustrated by the law of the Hebrew slave, given in Exodus 21. A Hebrew who became a slave had to be set free in the seventh year. If he came in by himself, he had to go out by himself; but if he came in married, his wife was free to go with him. If he came in single, and was permitted to marry, and his wife had borne him sons, then the wife and children belonged to the master, but he could go free.

Provision was made that if the man should plainly say, "I love my master, my wife, and my children; I will not go out free," he could remain for life. The text says, "for ever."

In such a case the man entered into a perpetual, willing servitude on the basis of love for his wife and children. If we apply this as in any way typical of Christ, it would mean that in His incarnation He came into the place of a bondservant, and this is the word used of Him in Philippians 2:7. His work was to reconcile the world to God. On His part, this involved the blood of atonement (Col. 1:20); but on the part of men, it required their being reconciled to God personally through the submission of faith, as indicated in II Corinthians 5:18-21.

During the millennial kingdom of Christ, also called the kingdom of the Son of man, Christ will subdue all things to Himself. Those who submit to Him willingly will be saved, while those who do not will be brought under judgment. It is then that Christ shall deliver up the kingdom to the Father, as we are told in I Corinthians 15. The eternal kingdom is called "the kingdom of God," or "the kingdom of the Father."

It might be expected that Christ, having fulfilled the mission for which He became incarnate, would give up His humanity and His place as servant. Instead, we read that "then shall the Son also himself be subject unto him that put all things under him, that God may be all in all." The fact that God is a Holy Trinity was not altered when Christ became incarnate, nor will it be by His willing subjection at the time referred to in the passage being considered. As I understand this passage, Christ will remain in manhood, leaving the sovereignty of that eternal kingdom with the Father.

198. How could Jesus pray to God if He was God? And when He died, was God dead? Who are the "us" in Genesis 1:26 ("And God said, Let us make man. . . .")?

The first and last of these questions are answered by understanding that God is a Holy Trinity, consisting of Father, Son, and Holy Spirit. The Lord Jesus, as God's Son, prayed to His Father. And in Genesis 1:26, it was God—Father, Son, and Holy Spirit—saying to one another, "Let us make man. . . ." The Holy Trinity planned creation in what has been called "the council chamber of eternity."

While the Lord Jesus in His deity is called "Son," this does not imply generation. Other Scriptures make it clear that He existed from all eternity with the Father and the Holy Spirit. He became a man in order to die, for without dying as a man He could not have delivered men from the penalty of sin. One of the main purposes of His incarnation was to become our Saviour by taking our place in the judgment.

Yet when He died, His divine being did not die. And when He died as a man, it was only His body which died. Scripture makes it clear that when *any* human being dies, it is the body which dies; the soul and spirit live on. Hence when Christ died we do not say that God died, though He who died on the cross was God. No finite mind can fully understand everything about the infinite God, but we can have some understanding of what is involved.

199. If God is one, how can a person blaspheme the Son of man without at the same time blaspheming the Holy Spirit?

We know that it can be done, because the Lord Jesus said in Matthew 12:32, "Whosoever speaketh a word against the Son of man, it shall be forgiven him: but whosoever speaketh against the Holy Ghost, it shall not be forgiven him, neither in this world, neither in the world [age] to come."

The unity of the Godhead is that of life and nature and attributes; but Father, Son, and Holy Spirit are distinct Persons. What is attributed to one of those Persons cannot always be said of another. Though the Son became man, we cannot say that the Father did. Neither can we say that the Holy Spirit became man, though He indwelt the Son and rested on Him.

Certainly, when a person blasphemes, he is sinning against God—Father, Son, and Holy Spirit. But the blasphemy against the Holy Spirit of which our Lord spoke was a particularly sinful act because of the deliberateness with which it was done. It was not done in weakness or ignorance, which might have been true of other types of blasphemy.

200. How can we understand that the three Persons of the Deity constitute one God?

We have already discussed that the oneness of God is partly in contrast with the multiplicity of heathen deities, each of whom was distinct from the other. The one living and true God, though subsisting as a Trinity, is the One who has made the universe and sustains it, and who will be the final Judge of all. We do not have to be concerned with other gods.

Various explanations of trinity in unity have been offered, such as the three colors constituting one American flag. We believe the best illustrations are those found in the Bible itself. For example, man is said to be made in the image and likeness of God, and man is a tripartite being—a trinity in unity. We are aware that many theologians contend that man is only bipartite, consisting of soul and body, though often those accepting this view distinguish between animal soul and rational soul. In I Thessalonians 5:23 the Apostle Paul, writing to the Thessalonian Christians, referred to their "whole spirit and soul and body."

Though soul and spirit can be separated from the body, this fact does not constitute a man two persons. At the martyrdom of Stephen, recorded in Acts 7 and 8, devout men carried Stephen to his burial. Yet Stephen had prayed, "Lord Jesus, receive my spirit." Where was Stephen? In one sense, he was in heaven; in another, he was in the grave. Both statements are true, yet Stephen was not two persons, he was one person.

The three Persons of the Holy Trinity share alike in the divine nature and attributes, have a common purpose, and always work in absolute harmony. We might illustrate this by calling attention to the way in which various members of the human body work harmoniously for the fulfillment of a common purpose. Another statement of Scripture is that "God is light" (I John 1:5). We are told that each ray of light consists of a luminiferous element, a calorific element, and an actinic element. Each performs a distinctive purpose, yet all, unitedly, constitute the ray of light. It does not make them three rays, yet there are three distinctive parts to the ray.

No created likeness can perfectly display God, but since these similes are given us in Scripture, we may find in them a comprehensible idea of how the God who made us consists of three distinct Persons who constitute one living and true God.

SCRIPTURE INDEX

TOPICAL INDEX

(See also the Table of Contents)

217